What do you do
when the inevitable
happens?

What do you do when the inevitable happens?

Maria Gonzalez

Copyright © 2020 by Maria Gonzalez.

Library of Congress Control Number: 2020913736
ISBN: Hardcover 978-1-5065-3345-2
Softcover 978-1-5065-3347-6
eBook 978-1-5065-3346-9

All rights reserved. No part of this book may be reproduced or transmitted in any form or by any means, electronic or mechanical, including photocopying, recording, or by any information storage and retrieval system, without permission in writing from the copyright owner.

The views expressed in this work are solely those of the author and do not necessarily reflect the views of the publisher, and the publisher hereby disclaims any responsibility for them.

Any people depicted in stock imagery provided by Getty Images are models, and such images are being used for illustrative purposes only. Certain stock imagery © Getty Images.

Scripture quotations marked KJV are from the Holy Bible, King James Version (Authorized Version). First published in 1611. Quoted from the KJV Classic Reference Bible, Copyright © 1983 by The Zondervan Corporation.

Print information available on the last page.

Rev. date: 03/08/2020

To order additional copies of this book, contact:
Palibrio
1663 Liberty Drive, Suite 200
Bloomington, IN 47403
Toll Free from the U.S.A 877.407.5847
Toll Free from Mexico 01.800.288.2243
Toll Free from Spain 900.866.949
From other International locations +1.812.671.9757
Fax: 01.812.355.1576
orders@palibrio.com
811195

CONTENTS

LIFE HAS A RESTART vii
A Letter to the Reader xix

Getting to Know Me 1
Untraditional proposal 4
Born Again 6
First Move to Ocala 8
Second Move to Ocala 10
AVM Burst Day 14
AVM SURGERY DAY 23
MAKING LEMONADE 28
SHANDS REHAB FACILITY 32
Avante at Ocala Rehab 42
Home Sweet Home 45
Cranioplasty 47
SAFETY FIRST 51
The Gall-Bladder Incident 52
Walking on Beach Sand 56
My AVM Daily Scriptures 58
Beginning with the End in Mind 67
The Eagle in Me 70
Planting the seed 76

Sink or Walk on Water 78
"Love her like Christ loves the church" 80
ONE IN A MILLION 83
The Heart of a Champion 85
The Preacher's Kids 89
My Advice 91
The Power of the Tongue 92
Feelings 93
Hit the Mountain 96
Re-wiring my brain 98
GRACE 102
My Husband Jorge's Reflection About My
AVM 115
My daughter-in-Law Cassy's Reflection
about my AVM 142
Moving Forward from the Disaster 148
My daughter-in-law Nichole's reflection
about my AVM 152
SAEBOFLEX 163

Conclusion 167

LIFE HAS A RESTART

What do you do when the inevitable happens?

The best way to answer this; is to share with you what I did. I went to my faith and found my comfort in His written word *"The Bible"*. Going through my AVM journey made me realize I had a lot to be thankful for; I am alive. My life started over; I had to learn to talk, get upper body balance, sit, stand, take steps, and walk (just like a child).

Every day is a new beginning and a blessing. I've gotten stronger. Holidays with family are precious. As I read His word; my life has purpose. Yes, there were dark moments, His word carried my husband Jorge and I through. It kept us sane through this insanity. My craziness was enough to cause us to default our faith, but God kept us through it. I thought about Matthew 14:13 – 21; where Jesus feeds the hungry crowd; by multiplying the fish and loaves. The Bible says he fed 5,000 hungry people. He took two fish and five loaves. First Jesus thanked the Father; then the miracle happened, the hungry got fed and there were leftovers. Every miracle Jesus did what he did first is thank the father. Then it hit me; I hadn't taken time to thank the Lord for allowing me to survive the AVM.

So, I like to begin my Journey expressing my gratitude and I know God takes care of the rest ("my healing").

Before you continue reading; thank you for taking time to read about my Journey.

TO THE LORD OF MY LIFE:

Father I thank you; you gave us your son Jesus Christ. Thank you for sending the Holy Spirit; that guides us to all truth and righteousness.

The truth is: I was lost like the Apostle Peter in the boisterous storm (**my AVM rupture & recovery**). I don't know where I'd be without you Lord! You pulled me through the biggest trial. You surrounded me with love, mercy, and compassion. Your presence was with me every day I sat down to write. I've never felt such overwhelming peace; especially when it came down to writing. Lord: you kept my sanity when I felt delirious. There's not a day that goes by that I don't think about the unmerited favor I've been given; your grace caught me. All I have is gratitude and appreciation for what you've done in my life.

TO MY LOVING HUSBAND:

There's no coincidence, chance, or luck between us. You're the man that God predestined for me. We're meant to be together. I'll always be thankful to God for what he's done, is doing, and will do in our lives. Thank you, my Angel, for your willingness to walk by my side. You saw me beautiful when I felt ugly, you were my strength when I was weak, and you pointed the way when I lost sight of who I am in Christ Jesus. Jorge I'll always love you!

TO MY DOCTORS:

Dr. Brian Hoh, I admire your dedication to the neurology profession. You saw the possibility when others thought it was impossible, and your 2017 neurology team was the most amazing group of individuals I've ever met. I believe God put you there the day my AVM ruptured; with the purpose of you taking medical care of me, so I could survive this valley in my life. I have respect, admiration, and appreciation for you.

I pray that God continues to open the eyes of your understanding, so you remain saving lives.

Dr. Jessica Ching, I value your dedication to reconstructive surgery and positive outlook through my recovery process. I have great admiration for you. I used to dislike looking in the mirror and seeing the void in my head because of the missing bone flap. At times, I felt so ugly. After my titanium mesh reconstruction, every time I look in the mirror, I see the woman I was before the AVM. Thank you isn't enough. I was blessed going in and blessed coming out.

TO MY SONS:

Boys you've grown and become amazing men. I'm so proud of you! Thank you for teaching me the true meaning of Philippians 4:13. Times got rough for me; and I'll never forget you were there to show me I could do it, and I did! Never forget with God **all things** are possible. All we need is mustard seed faith.

TO MY DAUGHTERS IN LAW:

Ladies each of you possess a special quality. I appreciate your encouragement through my AVM journey. I've always tried to lead by example. I wanted to be for you an example of the Proverbs 31 woman.

I think I succeeded!

TO MY PARENTS:

Dad and Mom thank you for your encouragement and help. I know this was difficult for you to see your only daughter (which you raised with love, care, and dedication) travel through such a punitive road. We know that God has bigger plans. He's not finished with me yet.

I love you!

TO MY BROTHER:

Wolfy, you're solely responsible for Jorge and me getting married. Thank you for bringing my Angel to me 34 years ago. Also, thank you for checking up on me daily. I looked forward to your phone call; there were times your phone call pulled me out of the gutter. Monica, Krizia, Izaiah, and Yamile, thank you for telling me every opportunity you had; that you're proud of me. Those words meant so much to me. I needed to hear that often through this journey.

TO MY PASTORS:

Pastors: Victorio and Betty Garcia-Barbon, thank you, for your commitment to the Gospel. The word of Grace you preach changed my life, and I've never been the same. I have appreciation, respect, and gratitude for you. You're "Champions for Christ". Through my recovery process, your messages were constantly on my mind. God used those to bring me out of this process. Pastor I still remember your positive thoughts during Sundays.

I know I'm an overcomer.

I'm a gladiator.

I'll never give up.

I must keep pressing forward to finish the race.

TO MY GRANDCHILDREN:

Each of you is my handsome prince and my beautiful princess. Your endless hugs and kisses lifted me when I was down.

Noah, I'll never forget the day you walked in to say hello and I was without a helmet. You ran out yelling," She has a hole in her head"! After that day, you kiss me on my left side. I know this wasn't easy for you and the rest of my grand babies.

TO BELLEVIEW ELEMENTARY SCHOOL:

Team Belleview (2016-2017) you're the most amazing team anyone could be a part of. God brought me to you with purpose. He knew I would need your support going through this valley. Thank you for your prayers, care, gift cards, and meals delivered to my door. Thank you for your words of encouragement. You inspired me to return to work both times, though the moment was short lived. Thank you isn't said enough to the most amazing team I've ever worked with.

<u>Tragedy hit and it affected us all,</u> my parents, husband, sons, daughters-in-law, and grandchildren. It didn't give us time to prepare, it was like picking up the broken pieces and restoring as you went.

A Letter to the Reader

Dear Reader:

I pray this book blesses you!

I wanted to give you a piece of me and share with you the tragedy that struck unexpectedly, its intention was to shatter my family's faith. Furthermore, I want to share with you the magnitude, love, and mercy of the God I serve. I came close to death; my family was so shattered they questioned God.

Why did God permit this to come to pass to my wife?

How did God consent that this happen to our mother?

Why did God allow this to occur to our mother in law?

How did God let this to come about to our momma (grandmother)?

She doesn't deserve this!

She's a Godly woman!

God in his infinite wisdom brought me back.

I'm a product of His word, faith, groaning and supplication before the throne of grace by my husband. My husband did what he knew as a pastor, he spoke the word to my spirit every day! While I lay in the hospital bed lifeless, and in a medically induced coma, my loving husband spoke God's written word to me.

When I awoke, I constantly thought about the sermons I heard on the importance of being equally yoked. An unequally yoked husband wouldn't have shared my faith. He probably would've left me in the hands of medical science, to face recovery on my own. My equally yoked and God-given husband shared my faith and made the best choice for my care, and when things got difficult, he slept on an inflatable mattress on the floor by my bedside. When the going gets tough, the tough pick up the Bible and begin quoting scriptures according to the need. I needed a miracle; I needed healing. So, my husband spoke healing scriptures, every day. It's the best gift I could've been given. I've been given unmerited favor and a second chance to witness God's glory.

To me God is real, and I know he listens to us in times of adversity. It doesn't matter what you're going through. I'm convinced, if you call out to God, pick up his word, and begin quoting scriptures according to your need, God is faithful. He will fulfill His word. My life would've been completely different if my husband hadn't picked up the word, called on the name of the Lord, and prayed for my life. I would've been in eternity. The prophet Isaiah said in Isaiah 55:9 - 13 His word, doesn't return void or empty, it accomplishes what it was sent to do. Every morning I awake, it's a new gift. I've been given the gift of life. Despite all I've been through, I still love God. I'm a witness of God's glory; to my church, friends, and family. It's my aspiration that this Journey awakens a desire in you to have a personal encounter with God, seek Him, and read his word. It'll be as Proverbs 3 says health to your flesh and strength to your bones!

Blessings,

Maria Gonzalez

I believe God Is

God means many things to numerous people. I want to define what God means to me. To accomplish it; I want to mention his attributes and a few scriptures.

Holy

Love

Merciful

Righteous

Sovereign

Omnipresent

Omniscient

Immutable

Holy:

Throughout the Bible, we're told God is Holy. He told Moses he's the Holy one of Israel. In the book of Isaiah God is called the **Holy One** over 30 times.

Isaiah 5:19

Isaiah 5:19 (NIV)

to those who say, "Let God hurry; let him hasten his work so we may see it. The plan of the Holy One of Israel— let it approach, let it come into view, so we may know it." (https://www.biblegateway.com)

Love:

The New Testament tells us approximately 20 times God is Love. It tells us God loves us unconditionally.

John 3:16

"For God so loved the world that he gave his one and only Son, that whoever believes in him shall not perish but have eternal life". (NIV)

Romans 5:8-9

"But God demonstrates his own love for us in this: While we were still sinners, Christ died for us.

[9] Since we have now been justified by his blood, how much more shall we be saved from God's wrath through him"! (NIV)

Merciful:

God's mercy endures forever. When I stop and think about my AVM; how it all came about unexpected. I must acknowledge that God is merciful. He has allowed me to survive the AVM, and little by little I'm getting stronger.

Deuteronomy 4:31

"For the Lord, your God is a merciful God; he will not abandon or destroy you or forget the covenant with your ancestors, which he confirmed to them by oath". (NIV)

2 Chronicles 30:9

"If you return to the Lord, then your fellow Israelites and your children will be shown compassion by their captors and will return to this land, for the Lord your God is gracious and compassionate. He will not turn his face from you if you return to him." (NIV)

Righteous:

God demonstrated his righteousness towards my family and me, by allowing me to survive the AVM. I can't forget the miracle God's done in my life and the opportunity I've been given. I've been given a second chance! To God be the Glory!

Romans 14:17

17 For the kingdom of God is not a matter of eating and drinking, but of righteousness, peace and joy in the Holy Spirit" (NIV)

1 Corinthians 1:30

"It is because of him that you are in Christ Jesus, who has become for us wisdom from God—that is, our righteousness, holiness and redemption". (NIV)

Sovereign:

Through this journey I've learned that God has a purpose and perfect timing for everything.

Ecclesiastes 3:1

"There is a time for everything, and a season for every activity under the heavens" (NIV)

He knows it all and every time we go through a process, God makes provisions for us, there's always a way out. As we spend time in His word; He shows us the way out. Psalm 82 says we're created like Him. When we give God control over our lives, He wants the best for us. Think about it; God allowed my AVM to burst in the perfect time. Medical science is advanced enough to keep me alive.

When we seek God; like my husband did for me. God gives us our desires according to His divine purpose. His purpose for us will be fulfilled; guaranteed. I realize sometimes lack of knowledge and refusal to accept His word; keeps us from His blessings. Not knowing His word holds us back.

Psalm 82:6-7

6 "I said, 'You are "gods"; you are all sons of the Most High.'

7 But you will die like mere mortals; you will fall like every other ruler."

We die like men and fall like every other ruler because of lack of knowledge of His word.

Our lives would be different if we adopt this mindset:

God said it!

I believe it!

I receive it!

I will act according to what His word says!

Colossians 1:17

"He is before all things, and in him all things hold together". (NIV)

Omnipresent:

The Bible states that God is everywhere.

He was with me when my AVM ruptured.

God was present in the surgery room.

He still is with me through my recovery.

The Lord never left me.

Proverbs 15:3

"The eyes of the Lord are everywhere,

keeping watch on the wicked
and the good". (NIV)

Jeremiah 23:23

"Am I only a God nearby, "declares the Lord,

"and not a God far away?

Omniscient:

Dictionary.com defines omniscient as: "having complete or unlimited knowledge, awareness, or understanding; perceiving all things". I believe God knew my AVM was going to rupture when I reached age 52. He made provisions for me to be medically taken care of, and he put medical experts in the right place, at the right appointed time.

Psalm 147:5

"Great is our Lord and mighty in power; his understanding has no limit". (NIV)

1 John 3:20

"If our hearts condemn us, we know that God is greater than our hearts, and he knows everything". (NIV)

Immutable:

God has made provision for my recovery every step of the way. He put excellent therapists in my path; He knew they would approach my recovery with an open mind and be willing to do what's best for me. My physical therapist has a master's degree in neurology (he convinced me that practice makes permanent).

My walking is permanent!

My Occupational therapist is a certified hand specialist (she introduced me to products that help promote hand function). She's one of the best hand therapists; in my opinion.

Numbers 23:19

"God is not human, that he should lie,

not a human being, that he should change his mind. Does he speak and then not act?

Does he promise and not fulfill? (NIV)

Getting to Know Me

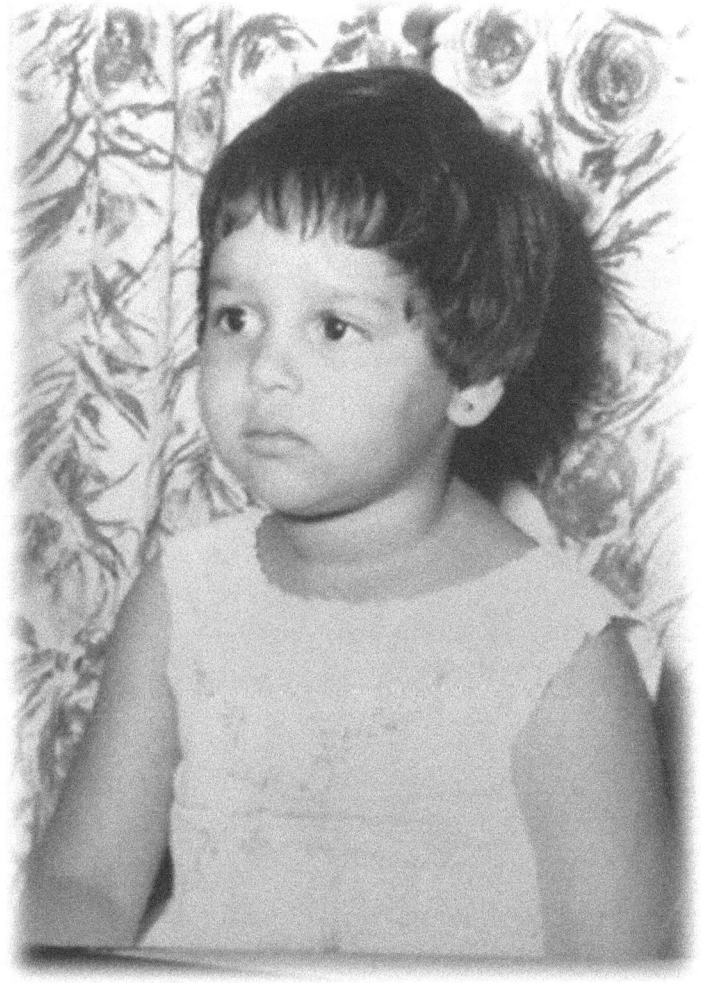

I was born April 9, 1965, in Havana, Cuba. My parents, Wilfredo, and Teresa Aguilar. My mother named me Maria de las Mercedes, because she was a Catholic when I was born. She thought of the virgin Mary and the virgin Mercedes.

My parents brought me to the USA on July 30,1969, through President Lindon Johnson's," Freedom Flight" program, I was 4 years old.

We went to live with my mother's sister in Key West, Florida, but my parents liked Miami, Florida; so, we moved to Miami. Once my parents got situated; we moved into a home, and I started school. My parents moved around a lot due to work; and due to their financial needs, I was constantly the new girl in class.

Once they settled in a permanent home; I went to Coral Terrace Elementary, and West Miami Middle. Both schools were in Miami, Florida.

When I was graduating West Miami middle school, my parents bought a house and I began attending South Miami Senior High.

Work got really slow for my father, and I took a part-time job at the mall, so I could help my parents. That job didn't work out for me; I applied at Kentucky Fried Chicken (KFC), and I was hired part-time, for evenings and weekends. It was at KFC; I met my husband Jorge. I graduated from South Miami Senior High June of 1983.

A few years later, Jorge and I met again because his parents bought a home 2 blocks away from my house. After a couple months of dating, we became boyfriend and girlfriend.

Untraditional proposal

Jorge and I had been boyfriend and girlfriend since December of 1985. In April 1986, Jorge's sister got married. I was invited to a family get together, the weekend after her wedding. Jorge's mother was talking about her adult children and how they're all married. Jorge blurts out in front of the entire family, "Maria and I are getting married in December on my birthday." At first, everyone thought he was joking. When I realized Jorge was serious; I was shocked. I asked Jorge, "exactly when you were planning on proposing?" He said, "I'm letting you know now that we're getting married in December on my birthday". I come from an extremely strict family; my younger brother was my chaperone. In my father's mind, the man with intentions about marrying me, first and foremost, needed to meet with the parents, to ask permission to become my boyfriend. Secondly, he'd formally do courtship at the house in front of the family for at least a year, and finally ask for my hand in marriage.

My father was upset and said, "What kind of man doesn't meet me or talks to me to ask for your hand in marriage"! I explained times changed.

Jorge wasn't someone I just met. I worked with him every week at KFC. We knew each other from work and had been dating for 4 months. So, when Jorge said he wanted to marry me, I was in love with him and said yes. My father didn't think that was a good reason and he was still upset. They weren't happy that Jorge broke their rules and traditions. My mother got involved in the wedding plans to keep the peace and began searching for wedding venues. My mother in law spoke to her pastor to see if he was available to do the wedding ceremony at their church. My parents decided to do a small wedding reception at their house, with only friends and family attending. Jorge and I married June 27, 1986. We have been married almost 34 years; we have three sons (Jorge Jr., Jonathan, and Joshua), three daughters in-law (Cassy, Lindsey, and Nichole), and six grandchildren (Gloria, Jonathan, Dahlia, Noah, Kyra, and Arianna). My grandchildren call me momma and they call Jorge papa. The girls, I call my beautiful princess, and the boys, I call my handsome prince. Who would've thought we'd be together this long? He is the best choice this girl made. As the years go by our love gets stronger in Christ Jesus our Lord!

<u>Born Again</u>

I became a born-again believer because the Lord delivered Jorge from cocaine and alcohol addiction (June 23, 1989). Since that day; we have been serving the Lord. I was so thankful for the miracle God had done. All I wanted to do; is support my husband. It was like starting over again with a new and improved husband, one that went to work every day and didn't show up to our home drunk. One that prayed and read the bible, a husband that got involved in church activities, he prayed with me and for me, a husband who would provide for our family through work.

Due to Jorge's cocaine and alcohol addiction I was full of hurt, pain, and resentment, but God always has a way of healing the wounded and the broken hearted. I loved my husband greatly, but I had a wounded spirit. God restored and rekindled our love. The Lord did this by reminding me of the scripture the pastor that married us read during our wedding ceremony. **Ruth 1:16** - "Don't urge me to leave you or to turn back from you. Where you go, I will go, and where you stay, I will stay". Your people will be my people and your God my

God". To me this was a big deal; I believe marriage is intended for husband and wife to grow old together. Marriage is teamwork. I believe marriage is till death do us apart".

This verse was a reminder from the Lord, and it was enough for me. That is when God healed all my hurt and pain. I was able to forgive Jorge and let go of the past. Every year on June 23rd, I buy a cake and we sing happy birthday to him. Jorge is 31 years of being delivered and drug free. We serve a mighty God! **In Him, all things are possible!**

Every opportunity I have, I witness to people the miracle God has done with my husband. We began to work with the youth at church. This led us to begin doing bible studies with the youth during Sunday service. We began doing activities with the youth. One Saturday, we went to Summerland Key, Florida and fished off their bridge. We began attending Christian concerts and events; did a Youth Rally Night and began to mentor church youth.

First Move to Ocala

Construction slowed down. We began having a difficult time providing the basic needs for our boys. God put in us a desire to move to Ocala. Jorge and I prayed about it; we took a couple of trips to Ocala.

We decided to put our condominium for sale, and the condominium sold quickly. We found a 3-bedroom 2-bathroom rental home in Ocala and did a 6-month lease. The get away from the city life was soothing therapy for Jorge and me. He found a good job framing, and I decided to be a stay at home mom, to care for our boys.

It was a matter of days; our parents began calling, telling us we needed to go back. We had moved too far away from family; it wasn't good for the kids to grow up without their grandparents and the family. When our lease expired in December; we moved back to Miami. We lived with my parents for a couple of months until we found a small duplex to rent.

The duplex had 2-bedrooms, and 1 bathroom with a small eat - in kitchen). All three boys slept in one room and shared one closet. The kids did not have space for their toys. They would share the yard with the neighbor's kids. They would play outside and while I did house chores, I'd watch them through my bedroom window.

Jorge and I kept thinking about Ocala. Rental and sales were low; it would be very affordable to buy our own home. The mortgage would be half the cost of rent. Ocala was quiet and peaceful, when compared to Miami. Housing was affordable.

Second Move to Ocala

Construction slowed down again (the joys of living in a city). I began working an evening temp job to help Jorge. When the assignment ended, Jorge began an evening part-time job. We could barely provide for our boys even with both of us working. Jorge and I did not want to be moving around looking for a bigger and cheaper home. We wanted to give the boys a stable home with a little more space. I moved around a lot and I did not like being the new girl in class. I knew how that felt and did not want our boys to go through that.

We began seeking the Lord and He led us to return to Ocala, Florida. We traveled to Ocala back and forth a few times until we found a home we could afford; we bought the home and returned to Ocala, FL on August 19, 1998, for the closing on our home.

We were so happy having a home that was ours and not rented; it was finally a piece of stability for our family, with a fenced in backyard for our boys to play in. Their own yard and not a yard shared with the neighbor's kids.

After being situated into our home, we visited various churches, and the Lord led us to start a group at our home.

The church we attended in Miami was beginning a book study; it was "The Purpose Driven Life" by Rick Warren. We began that book study. The group began to grow, and the group began to express they wanted more than a book study; they wanted a pastor, they wanted a church. God has a way of doing things according to his divine purpose.

Finally, the time came when the group told Jorge, they saw him as their pastor. After a Sunday service, the group prayed together and ordained Jorge as their pastor. I began to do the paperwork to open the non-profit corp., "**Where the Eagles Soar Ministry, Inc.**" was electronically filed with the state of Florida on August 23, 2006. **Our Mission Statement was:** *"Changing Lives One Family at a Time"*. Our sons invited their neighborhood friends and the group grew.

When our boys grew and became adults, Jorge and I were mostly alone; we had each other, and we became best friends.

The group continued to grow (at one point I was accommodating 45 people in my family room every Sunday). I felt the need to be prepared and enrolled in Liberty University's online program to pursue a master's degree in Pastoral Counseling, because I had a desire to help people.

I graduated from Liberty University and my degree was conferred in September of 2009.

There still was a great need in the ministry, some of the members were going through family problems. I used the knowledge gained from my pastoral counseling degree; to freely counsel and help people overcome family problems. Later, my duties became, doing worship music on power point, light bookkeeping, and I taught book studies on Wednesday nights. Some of the book studies were War Room, Soul Detox, God's Not Dead, and the women in the bible. The women in the bible; was the book study we were doing when my AVM ruptured.

I worked for 18 years at Marion County's public-school system; and taught for 14 out of those 18 years. I looked forward to coffee with Jorge every afternoon after work. We would sit on the sofa and discuss the workday, plan church movie nights and our vacations together.

If you told me my life was about to go through turmoil; I would have called, you a liar. We were truly blessed and full of joy! I have a great partner; and he is my best friend! We are in ministry together and our focus has always been ministry.

The inevitable happened; I suffered an unexpected AVM rupture.

AVM Burst Day

April 6, 2017 was my average stressful workday. It was after students dismissed, my fourth-grade co-workers and I were discussing students and sharing best practices. Our conversation shifted; we began to share testimonies about our own kids and their teenage year's struggles. I was standing by the POD door, sharing stories about my boys. I remember, it happened suddenly, I felt as if my brain was shaking, my vision blurred, I felt this intense pressure inside my head, and my legs grew weak. I thought I was going to drop to the ground. I told Amy (my team teacher) I was not feeling well, and I was going to my desk to sit down and see if this went away. I remember looking at the lesson plans I was typing on my computer, and I could not read anything because my vision was blurred.

Amy brought over some smarties candy and suggested my sugar might be low and sometimes it helps to eat something sweet. I ate all the smarties and I did not feel better. Everything looked three dimensional, extremely bright, and bubble like. Things appeared as if they were floating around. My vision was sensitive to light.

I knew something was terribly wrong; but I didn't know what. I couldn't think. I remember shaking my head to see if it would help me re-gain my eyesight balance.

Sitting at my desk; I couldn't think, read, reason, or see clearly. I looked at the clock on the wall and thought, I must get home because if Jorge gets home, and I'm not there, he's going to worry about me.

I walked slowly to the car; my legs felt like noodles, I got in the car and put on my seatbelt. I called Jorge to tell him what happened to me.

Jorge's father had suffered a stroke and Jorge was taking him home from Avante at Ocala Rehab that day. Jorge said he just finished helping his father and was on the way home.

He told me to sit down, relax and try not doing anything until he got home.

He thought I was too stressed out from work and believed I needed to rest. I hung up the phone and prayed the way home for strength to make it there. Those two blocks I had to drive; felt like miles. My feeling was; if I just make it home, I'll be fine.

Feeling disoriented and air headed; I thanked the Lord that I made it home. Parked and got out of the car; slowly took a few steps to the handicap ramp, then held on to the rail and walked up to the door and opened it. Once inside our home I locked the door; walked to the sofa and sat down.

My head was throbbing; I felt nauseous and put a decorative pillow behind my head. Leaned back; put my feet up on the sofa and began to fall asleep. Jorge got home; he woke me up, took one look at me, and said let's go to the urgent care. The urgent care was packed; the reception area said I had an hour wait before I would be seen by a doctor. We sat down to wait for the doctor; I began to feel worse and said to Jorge "don't feel very well, and can't wait long, please take me to the emergency room at the hospital. Jorge told the reception area we 're leaving to the emergency room at the hospital. We got in the car, Jorge began to drive towards the exit, and when he was approaching the stop sign that leads to the main road", I told him stop the car and then opened the car door and began throwing up. Jorge took me to Monroe Regional Hospital's Emergency, and it was packed like the urgent care center, we were told there is a two hour wait. We take a seat to wait to be seen by a doctor. My headache grew worse and I could not hold my head up, I remember leaning my head forward and supporting it with my right arm and hand. At some point, I leaned on Jorge's shoulder, and closed my eyes. I remember throwing up on the floor. At that point, I thought I would be transferred to a room in the emergency area, but no I still had to wait. Hospitals can be so insensitive with people. Finally, the time came where I was placed in a room in the emergency area, pending to be seen by a doctor. They gave me medication for my headache, and it made me fall asleep.

I recall having silent talks with God; asking him to please take care of me, I didn't feel right.

Next thing I know, I'm surrounded by doctors wanting to transport me to Shands Hospital in Gainesville, Florida. They're telling me; they have a neurosurgeon on-board at Shands and he's waiting for me. I said wait a minute! You can't take me anywhere, and I have my family out there in the lobby waiting for me.

As they wheeled me to the ambulance transport, I'll never forget Jorge's face, with tears in his eyes saying," this isn't fair you're a good woman you don't deserve this.

I interrupted him, "stop it!

Stop it right now! You have your testimony for God, and I have nothing. This is my testimony for God. Everything happened so fast that I didn't have time to think.

I was in an ambulance transport, about to be transported to Shands Hospital, and it didn't occur to me that my condition was critical.

Monroe Regional Hospital was in a big hurry to get me to Shands and they didn't ask Jorge if he wanted to come with me in the ambulance. There was a paramedic riding in the back with me. After the transport took off, it was God and I in that transport, I ignored the paramedic, and my focus was God. I closed my eyes and began my silent talk with the Lord. I don't know what is wrong with me; but Lord my trust is you. Father you know all things and you know what is wrong with me. Please take care of me; I need to arrive to the hospital.

When the transport arrived at Shands hospital; Dr. Brian Hoh was waiting for me outside on the sidewalk. He shook my hand; introduced himself and his neurology team. He smiled and said," are you ready?" I responded, yes. Somehow, I felt relieved to know that I was at Shands Hospital. Dr. Hoh's smile was warm and comforting; it made me feel at peace. Which reminds me, Jesus said this about our burdens in Matthew 11:28 "Come to me, all you who are weary and burdened, and I will give you rest". (NIV)

My thought was: I had arrived at the place where I would find rest in Christ Jesus. God's in control of my life and my trust is in Him. My view about the AVM is: Ecclesiastes chapter 3 mentions there is a time for everything.

My AVM went undetected until it ruptured when I was 52 years old. God knew there was going to be a neurosurgeon named Dr. Brian Hoh, who would step up to the challenge and be prepared to do the surgery that saved my life and brought me back. God used Dr. Brian Hoh to take medical care of me in a way the Lord knew I would recover.

Here I am recovering!

Throughout my years as a believer, I believe in a miracle working God. A God that if we dwell in His word and seek Him. He will give us our desires, according to His divine purpose. I believe in a God who delivers, heals, and restores. It is my belief when medical science can't do anything for you; God can. I feel where science ends and can offer no solution; God takes over, He gives the doctor wisdom and becomes the solution.

As I was wheeled into the hospital on the ambulance transport bed; the neurology team followed me through the hospital. I reached a hospital room and Dr. Hoh explained I suffered a brain bleed, there was a procedure he needed to do and consent paperwork to sign.

Next minute: I was surrounded by medical staff, with everyone having a procedure to explain. At that point I was overwhelmed by everything and asked, where is my husband? They said he is on his way. I replied, when he gets here discuss this with him, I give him the authority to make all decisions for me and sign the necessary paperwork.

Jorge was left in charge of making decisions and honestly, emotionally it was difficult for me to make any decisions. I felt in complete peace and trusted that my God-given husband would make the best choice for me. My poor husband! What a burden to bear! He was left alone to make life-threatening decisions for me.

We were informed the CT scan showed I suffered an AVM rupture and there is a small trace of blood in my brain. My AVM looked like a giant spider-web! The procedure Dr. Hoh wanted to do is an angiogram; it was scheduled to be done on April 7, 2017. Most of the time; the AVM can be treated with the angiogram.

Unfortunately, my AVM was so big that it couldn't be treated with the angiogram. The AVM was going to be surgically removed. Imagine; first I went through an angiogram, and now I was facing brain surgery. The surgery was set for April 10, 2017 and after the surgery; I was going to be placed in a medically induced coma, until all the swelling from brain surgery came down. I spent my birthday at Shands Hospital in ICU. My family had special permission to bring a cake without candles. I was so happy to see everyone.

My cellphone is where you'll find stored my favorite songs. That day after eating a piece of my birthday cake, I sang the song "Holy Spirit" by Francesca Batistelli (my favorite song). As I lay in the hospital bed singing my favorite song; tears started rolling down my cheeks. It was a short-lived moment; because my heart rate went up and they sent everyone out.

In my mind I wanted God's presence there regardless of the religious background of the medical staff. I serve Him and I needed His presence there. It doesn't matter what we have done, God is love. He knows our thoughts. At that moment I knew I needed God more than ever.

AVM SURGERY DAY

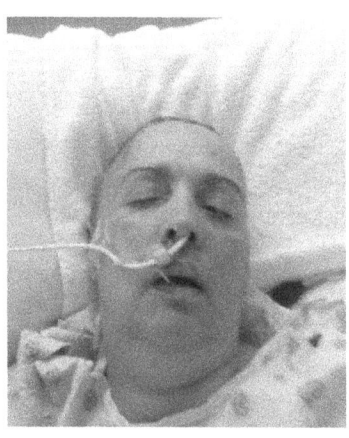

April 10, 2017; I was so nervous I wouldn't talk. My husband said, on the way to surgery, they wheeled me in a transport bed by the family waiting room. I looked at him with worried eyes; and didn't say a word. When I reached the surgery room; they placed me on a surgery bed, I looked around and realized only medical staff surrounded me.

At that moment I felt a little afraid; I remember thinking; "this is it" Lord!

They put a mask on my face (it looked like the mask used for nebulizer treatments), it was for the anesthesia. I hesitated a bit and everyone was telling me to breathe. A million thoughts were going through my head; anxiety, fear, worry, etc. I remember, calling out to the Lord one more time. While being told to breathe I wanted to speak to the Lord before I went under. I said to the Lord; Father I know that when Science ends, you take over. Lord, I do what Jesus did; I give you my life, I trust you will take care of me, God I give up my soul, I give it to you, please take care of me. The last thing I remember saying; Lord I have a room full of people out there waiting for me. Please bring me back. I want to come back.

I went to sleep.

At some point, I had a vision or dream, and saw an Angel at my bedside, the Angel looked like a gladiator. He was tall, strong, and muscular. He carried me and I was instantly transported to heaven. He sat me down on an elongated sofa. I looked around and everything was gold, the floor, and the sofa. It was so bright. I saw two figures and glory was all around them; they were dressed in gold, I tried to see their faces, but the light that shone from their faces was so bright, it blinded me, I had to look away. I knew I was in heaven, and in the presence of the Lord. It was so peaceful; I was so relaxed and carefree. It felt like time stood still. I asked one question.

Is it time?

Both said, "No, I'm sending you back because I heard his cry and pointed down to earth". At that moment, I knew they were referring to Jorge. This reminds me of Jesus in the garden of gethsemane, Luke 22:42 -43 42 "Father, if you are willing, take this cup from me; yet not my will, but yours be done." 43 An angel from heaven appeared to him and strengthened him". (NIV)

I was spared from the cup of death and sent back to witness God's Glory; to tell everyone about my AVM story (my miracle!).

As I was coming back, I could hear the doctor calling my name, Maria! Maria! He told the other medical staff that was with him "She's awake". "She said she has a hard time waking from anesthesia". I remember looking at the ceiling and seeing it covered with Angels. **Psalm 91:11 – 12 -** For he will command his angels concerning you to guard you in all your ways; they will lift you up in their hands, so that you will not strike your foot against a stone". (NIV) It was so bright; there was a glow around the doctor's head; this made him look like an Angel.

It's a miracle! God brought me back!

I'm a miracle; and did nothing to deserve this. It is a gift from God. His mercy and grace transcend all understanding.

The days that followed, I tried to remember what happened after that moment and I can't. I can remember specific events but not everything.

My family said I spoke in sign language (I never took sign language!). They said I'd signal with my hands I love everyone. This is something I taught my grandkids when they were little.

I remember spending countless hours scanning my brain, and I began putting bits and pieces together. **Psalm 91:14 – 16 (NIV)** "Because he set his love on Me, therefore I will save him; I will set him [securely] on high, because he knows My name [he confidently trusts and relies on Me, knowing I will never abandon him, no, never]. 15 He will call upon Me, and I will answer him; I will be with him in trouble; I will rescue him and honor him. With a long life I will satisfy him, and I will let him see My salvation". The Lord heard my request.

MAKING LEMONADE

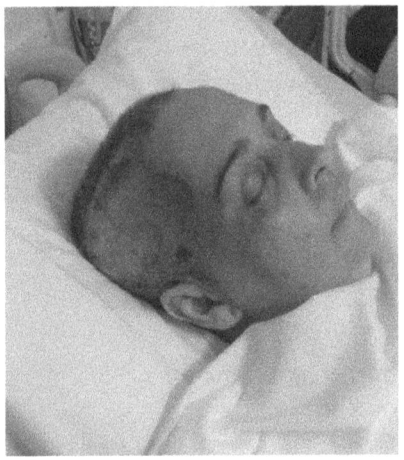

Have you heard the proverbial phrase when life gives you lemons you make lemonade?

Well it's my turn to make lemonade!

I was taken off the breathing machine and brought back from the medically induced coma. I was having difficulty breathing; they strengthened my lungs, by giving me breathing treatments hourly.

I felt like a computer booting up for the first time. The computer spends a long time organizing all its files and doing updates. Who am I?

What happened to me?

Where am I?

Why am I missing a piece of my skull?

Why am I in pain and can't move?

The first time my family came to see me it was devastating; I didn't recognize them. When Jorge walked in; I knew him but didn't know he is my husband. At first, I thought; ooh I know this handsome man, but who is he? I asked my mother; who are these people?" She said, "Maria this is your husband and family". My response: I don't remember them.

The days that followed I experienced brokenness; hurt and pain. I felt like Jesus felt in **Matthew 27:46** "About three in the afternoon Jesus cried out in a loud voice, "Eli, Eli, [a] lema sabachthani?" (which means "My God, my God, why have you forsaken me?"). (NIV)

I thought about it and couldn't understand why I had to go through this. It was my understanding; I'd go through this surgery to remove my AVM, and when the wound healed, I would be my normal self again.

Unfortunately, my expectations were shattered. Dr. Hoh did a bypass of the AVM; the bypass was unsuccessful, and I suffered a stroke. The stroke left my left side paralyzed; it affected my peripheral vision; my face was twisted. It left me an emotional mess with a million questions. Kept scanning my brain; what did they do to me during surgery that I can't remember people important to me (my husband and my family). My heart was torn. I felt abandoned by the Lord. For days I kept going back and forth, scanning my brain as much as I could, until it wore me out from too much thinking…

Why did God allow this horrible thing to happen to me?

What did I do to deserve this?

Surely, I must have done something wrong. Scanned my brain to see if I remember doing something that brought about this horrible situation and I would hit a dead end every time. Started reasoning; don't abuse alcohol, don't like drinking. Never used drugs. I felt so broken. Prayed and felt alone. There were days I felt like Abraham talking to the Lord. Here I am Lord. Yes Lord. Some Days I felt like Job going through that terrible disease. It was as if the Lord didn't hear my call. Everything was blurred and doubled, which meant reading the bible difficult. Most days I felt unarmed and insane.

The day I shared with my daughter in law Nichole about not recognizing my husband and thinking he was handsome the first time he came to see me. Nichole said, "Thank God momma you thought he was handsome. Can you imagine telling poppa after thirty years of marriage, that you don't like him anymore"?

SHANDS REHAB FACILITY

After the surgery I spent approximately 20 days in Shands ICU for recovery, their care was impeccable and the hospital recommended Shands rehab, because I needed ongoing therapy.

The stroke left me weak and in pain. At Shands Rehab, I would hear the nurses talking among themselves about patients that suffered a stroke; how their spouses weren't willing to take care of them and they filed for a divorce. These conversations happened often and that stayed ringing in my head.

Seeing my condition left me thinking; what if my husband feels this is too much for him? What if he doesn't want me anymore? Maybe these nurses are right.

When Jorge came into my room, I said to him, sit down we need to talk. Then told him, "Please tell me our 30 years of marriage meant something to you and they weren't in vain. "Please tell me we're in this together. "Promise me you aren't going to give up on me and leave me. He looked at me and responded, "Girl! You don't know what I've been through"! "You were practically dead, I almost lost you". "Don't worry I'm not going anywhere".

The days that followed therapy began. The stroke affected my balance and they'd use a gait belt to secure me to the wheelchair; otherwise I'd fall over. I had to learn to sit; my occupational therapist worked with me daily on regaining my upper body balance. She came every morning with an assistant; they'd sit me on the bed, balanced me until I was sitting straight, and when they let me go, I'd fall over. I developed a little humor, and they'd laugh when they hear me say catch me, falling, falling. They gave me food through a feeding tube.

One late afternoon, a CNA came in (Jorge, my son Joshua, and my daughter in law Nichole were there visiting); I didn't want to get up from the chair to be transferred to my bed; Jorge went to help her, she told him to back away. She forced me out of my seat, picked me up, and she threw me on the bed. My left stroke leg dropped; I suffered a groin tear. It set me back from recovery and left me in pain. That night Jorge went to a local

Walmart; he bought an inflatable mattress and spent 28 days sleeping in my room making sure they took good care of me. Physical Therapy was so painful! It hurt to stand and take a step. Every time I tried to take a step my left knee felt like it was popping out of the joint, and I felt pain, along with the feeling like I am falling. It came to the point; I didn't want to do physical therapy. I was refusing from doing therapy and they brought a psychologist to talk to me. He tried to tell me that my pain was in my head.

The psychologist insisted it was my brain sending messages of pain; due to the stroke I suffered. They were so focused on making me walk; Physical therapy wrapped bed sheets around my hips and legs, they forced me to stand. Two physical therapy assistants would help me stand, while the physical therapist would pull one leg at a time and force me to take steps. All that mattered is to have me walking in what they called "time window". They kept telling me it was important for me to walk in the window once the window passes; I missed the opportunity for recovery and walking. They missed the point. I was a human being with emotions and going through something I had never been through. I went from being a woman that took care of her husband and sons, to a woman in a wheelchair incapable of taking care of herself. I felt like I was in a hopeless situation with no way of fixing the problem. My face was all twisted, my arm paralyzed, I couldn't eat independently, my husband would feed me (like a child). The nurses fed me bowless feedings through a tube. It didn't occur to them that my injury was getting in the way of my recovery. The psychologist continued trying to convince me; it was all in my head and it wasn't real. I argued I was in pain and began to cry, they finally saw I wasn't giving up my argument, and Jorge was getting upset of seeing me go through pain, so they ordered an MRI. Twenty days of arguing "I'm in pain" and they finally decide to do an MRI, the MRI showed a mass or shadow, it wasn't clear.

We began hearing the nurses say comments like; let's hope it's nothing serious (like cancer), because there's a shadow in your MRI, it looks like a ball, it could be a mass, we don't know. I was referred to orthopedics; the orthopedic did an x-ray, looked at my MRI. He couldn't understand what happened to me, because no one explained anything to him, the incident wasn't documented in my chart (even though my husband reported it to the head nurse). He said he has seen these tears in people who would've had a motorcycle accident. Jorge told the doctor, about the incident at the rehab, with the CNA. He said that explains it. He said I suffered a tear, and had bursitis on my hip, and a Heterotopic ossification was beginning to form. The way that the orthopedic doctor explained it, the brain will send calcium to the injured area and it will begin to heal. He suggested for me to keep doing therapy and it will eventually heal. I was given a hip shot to help with bursitis and the pain, and I was told time will allow my injury to heal. It has been over three years; I still can't do knee lifts.

I'm still limited in my stretches, all due to the carelessness of a CNA. There are days that my inner thigh hurts, especially after therapy. I've continued doing therapy exercises at home and refuse to give up! Be prepared to be there for your loved one, if they ever need to be placed in any health facility, hospital, rehab center, nursing home, you name it. You are the only one that can advocate for your loved one!

When I went for speech therapy my first question to the therapist was, do I talk slow? "Is my speech delayed"? She said, "no, you suffered a stroke, it's going to take time, and you're going to get your speech back. I lost so much, and it was heart breaking. It pleased me to see my ability to read wasn't lost, Speech therapy brought in a magnifying glass.

They taught me to scan from left to right when reading. We practiced ordering food from a menu. I would do timed readings. I loved speech therapy, more than physical therapy. Physical therapy produced pain and that was the last thing I wanted to do. With my brokenness, I acquired a new Physical Therapy vocabulary; torture, unbearable, devastating, agony and excruciation.

Every morning when Jorge and I woke up, he read me healing scriptures, and he'd pray with me. My husband became my counselor and to think I was the one with the pastoral counseling degree.

Jorge was patient, kind, soothing, the elixir to my craziness.

1 Corinthians 13:4-7 "Love is patient, love is kind. It does not envy, it does not boast, it is not proud. 5 It does not dishonor others, it is not self-seeking, it is not easily angered, it keeps no record of wrongs. 6 Love does not delight in evil but rejoices with the truth. 7 It always protects, always trusts, always hopes, always perseveres. (NIV)

I'm so blessed and thankful, my AVM ruptured when it did. It ruptured at a time when, Jorge and I reached maturity in our faith. My husband preaches the good news, he loves God, and he knows scripture. Can you imagine what would've happened to us, if my AVM would've ruptured before God delivered Jorge from cocaine and alcohol addiction?

I embraced negativity again, and it began to consume me. Then, I began letting all the hurt in and only wanted to be medicated so I'd be numb.

Jorge noticed it and he began to monitor my pain medicine. That's why he's my God-given husband. He loved me enough to know what's best for me. He experienced addiction and kept me from traveling down that road.

It came to a point I just wanted to be numb and asleep. Didn't care about anything just wanted to be numb. Reality; there's no such thing.

The pain was covered by drowsiness and sleep. Medicine didn't heal my condition or pain, it would Band-Aid the symptoms and cause problems. I had difficulty doing therapy medicated; it made me drowsy and I'd fall asleep sitting on my wheelchair. My stroke recovery was slow and frustrating because I wanted a time frame of recovery and no one could give me an answer. Being a fourth-grade math teacher; I was trained to be data driven and I wanted the data to the time frame for full recovery. All they'd say is we don't know it depends; everyone is different, you need to keep doing therapy and don't give up. That's what I didn't want to hear; It bothered me they couldn't provide solid answers.

After breakfast, Jorge would take me out to the atrium to spend time together. I loved going out to the atrium; it had all kinds of plants. There were squirrels in the atrium, and I loved watching the squirrels. One morning I asked Jorge; "Why did God do this to me?

My husband said, "God didn't do this to you". We're going through a process and I'll be with you every step of the way. You're going to be fine. I'd say, "do you promise". He'd reply, "I promise".

The days that followed were still full of negativity and many questions. I'd ask; how can you love me like this? Jorge would respond; "I love you just the way you are". Well, I don't feel beautiful. You're beautiful inside. What if I die? You're not going to die. You're here, aren't you?

God brought you back for a purpose; you're here to give him glory. Am I a burden? You're not a burden. Why do I feel like a burden?

You're not and don't ever think that. There'll come a day you'll get stronger and be able to do things more independent, but for now you're my wife and I love you; I'm here to take care of you. Honestly, I don't mind taking care of you.

Mother's Day came. I remember my family cooked a delicious meal. They brought enough food to feed an army! We spent some time together and I rejoiced knowing that my family was there for me. My boys did what I expected them to do.

Before the AVM, I'd plan a get together on Mother's Day, so that the entire family could spend time together. Everyone cooked something and we came together to eat our meal. That Mother's Day at the rehab was special; my family made it special. We sat at picnic tables around the atrium. I was overjoyed to be with my family.

<u>Avante at Ocala Rehab</u>

Shands rehab transferred me to Avante at Ocala Rehab.

Jorge wanted a place closer to family and home. Shands Rehab was about an hour away from home and family. Jorge remembered his father was placed at Avante; during his stroke recovery, and he asked if they would transfer me to Avante.

The day Jorge drove me to Avante; it felt so good to be out on the road. I felt normal. Shands rehab had strict rules. Patients weren't allowed to leave the facility. I felt like a prisoner, at times. There were days I wanted to go out for a drive with my husband, but I had to settle for the atrium.

At Avante, I was discharged from speech therapy during my first session, because my cognitive abilities were there. After that, Speech therapy came a couple of days a week, to do exercises to strengthen my facial muscles and correct my facial left side.

Physical therapy focused on walking and strengthening my left leg. I remember my first session with my physical therapist at Avante. I began by complaining and telling him; I can't", it hurts, I don't feel well. He responded," "I don't know what you're complaining about. We're going to do sit to stands and you know how to do those, don't you"? I'd say yes. He'd answer, "Good, let's go". Next thing you know, I'm doing sit to stands. My therapist has a master's degree in neurology. He's the only therapist that was able to get inside my head and break me from the wall of fear I'd built. Fear? Yes, because of my experience of being pushed to do things that hurt (due to the injury I suffered when I wasn't mentally prepared, by my physical therapist at Shands Rehab).

He began with sit to stand and before you know it; I was working on taking steps at the parallel bars, I began using a hemi-walker to walk around the physical therapy gym and began gaining strength, I was so proud when I was given a four-point cane. Worked daily at therapy and made progress! I've always said practice makes perfect and my therapist would respond," No, practice makes permanent". I'd say no, no, no. I'm a teacher and I know. For once I agree with him. Practiced every weekday walking and I can walk! I've made so much progress, now I'm able to walk short distances without a cane, my husband insists on walking beside me to make sure I'm safe. I CAN WALK!

<u>With God, all things are possible!</u>

Occupational therapy at Avante focused on my arm and hand.

I loved Avante; they allowed me to check out on Sundays and come home for church service. When it was time to go back to Avante I would cry, because I wanted to be home with my husband. I missed home and missed my husband. This wife wanted to be next to her God-given man.

A wife's place is right beside her husband!!

Home Sweet Home

Jorge decided to bring me home and become a full-time caregiver, because having to travel back and forth between home and Avante was taking a toll on him. Truth be told; I would cry every night when it was time for him to leave. He didn't like to see me cry.

I was discharged from Avante and approved for outpatient therapy. The doctor ordered a wheelchair, an adjustable bed, and my father gave me the bedside commode he had from his knee surgery.

The first few days were rough, but I was so happy to be home. There were nights I lay in bed and think. This is awesome! I'm finally home with my husband! I'm where I belong!

Jorge barely slept keeping an eye on me; every move I'd make in my sleep, Jorge would ask," are you feeling alright"? When he began to fall asleep, I'd wake him up because I had to use the bathroom. I was like having an infant, where parents barely get sleep. Initiated to embrace the negativity again and began with the questions. Do you think I'm a load? My husband would respond," You're not a load". I can't do things alone, don't let you sleep, and think I'm a load. He'd say, "Maria I love you and don't mind taking care of you". "I'm here for you and want to take care of you. Let me take care of you".

Jorge would take afternoon naps with me so he could catch up with much needed sleep.

Cranioplasty

July 18, 2017 was the day where I'd get my bone flap back! Missing my bone caused me to be off balance; lots of noise gave me headaches and made me feel like I had this intense pressure inside my head. I was constantly off balance and felt like my brain was floating.

My bone flap insertion and recovery were more painful than usual.

The doctor explained to Jorge that they had to scalp me to be able to pull some skin over the flap. They put drain tubes and a fluid collection bottle at the end of the drain tubes. One of the nurses that took care of me on the neuro floor called the bottle "Gusher", for some reason, it reminded her of a kid's drink commercial.

After surgery I remember having pain in the back of my neck, around my spine. The doctor said it was meningitis. I freaked out and said, doc all my life I've never had meningitis. He laughed gently and assured me I didn't have meningitis per se. This was because of the surgery, and it was normal.

The day of discharge came, and my discharge doctor saw I had some stiches behind the right ear that needed to be fixed. He re-did those stitches and I was sent home. In my mind this was the missing piece, and in due time, it would all heal. The discharge orders said to continue therapy as instructed by the doctor.

A month later was my follow-up appointment with Dr. Hoh's office. The doctor that attended me that day; was the same doctor that discharged me from the hospital, he looked at my stitches and said the stitches needed to be re-done again. I wasn't prepared for the pain I endured that day. He gave me local anesthesia, the stitches and surrounding area were cleansed, and removed to be redone. Anesthesia was short and at some point; I could feel the needle piercing through my skin. The pain was intolerable. The doctor kept telling me to hold on a little bit more. When the doctor was finished; he said I behaved like a champ. Jorge thanked the doctor and he wheeled me out. Midway through the hospital lobby, I remember crying and yelling at Jorge "I hate you because you keep bringing me here, you watch them hurt me and do nothing"! I hate being put through pain!

When we were on our way home; I realized I hadn't been fair to Jorge, he wasn't a medical expert and tried the best he could to take care of me, by making sure I came to my follow-up visits. The trip home I felt so bad for yelling at Jorge and knew what I did was wrong. Once those words came out, I couldn't stop the damage or take back what I said. What's done is done and I did plenty. I apologized to Jorge for my outburst; thank God he understood me.

 In time everything healed, and I was at home recovering.

 On August 16, 2017; I asked Jorge to look at the back of my head because, I felt it was throbbing. Jorge looked and called Dr. Hoh's office. The nurse practitioner discovered a stitch was left in and a pus bubble formed. This burst in the doctor's office when she removed the stitch.

 It ended up being an emergency surgery and my bone flap was removed and discarded, because it was infected. I was completely devastated; they referred me to an infectious diseases doctor and the doctor ordered a PICC Line.

The lab results came back stating that the infection was environmental.

When they remove your bone; it's frozen and stored to prevent it from getting contaminated. When it's time to place it back; they need to thaw it. There's always risk of infection; and I won that prize.

They placed me on six weeks of antibiotics through the PICC line twice a day. Before this event, I was getting stronger at therapy, this set me back from making progress. When I healed from the bone-flap removal, I went back to Avante Rehab because the PICC line was something new for Jorge; he didn't want to make mistakes and wanted to keep me safe.

During one of my follow up visits, Jorge expressed his concerns to Dr. Hoh. He said I would be referred to a plastic surgeon that specializes in reconstructive surgery.

SAFETY FIRST

Jorge read the PICC line brochure and discovered safety protocol wasn't being followed by some of the nursing staff at Avante rehab; to keep me safe. Simple things like wearing gloves, wiping ports with alcohol; and locking the ports so bacteria couldn't get in. This was critical because if it were contaminated, it would go straight to my heart. He started to question everything and came to the decision; it was best to bring me home to take care of me. Like I said before; you're the only one who can advocate for a loved one and keep them safe.

Jorge spoke to my primary care doctor and he agreed to discharge me from Avante, and I could continue my recovery at home. I would come to Avante for outpatient therapy. Jorge agreed to continue doing my antibiotic infusions. Avante removed my feeding tube before my discharge, per doctor's order. I needed to follow up with the infectious diseases doctor. My surgery incision healed well, and the lab-work looked great, recovery was looking great too! The infectious diseases doctor said it was time to remove the PICC line, she discharged me and placed me on an oral antibiotic as a precaution.

The Gall-Bladder Incident

I was doing outpatient physical therapy and began complaining of pain in my core. Blamed my physical therapist; I thought he was making me work too hard. Next thing I know, the pain was intolerable, and it was an emergency visit to the hospital. My gallbladder went bad and had to be surgically removed. Underwent surgery and spent three days in ICU with antibiotics through an IV. I was discharged and sent home with an oral antibiotic. The ICU nurse removed my drain tube before leaving the hospital. I had a follow up with the surgeon two weeks later. All healed well and I was discharged. The time came where I'd need my bone flap replaced.

Dr. Hoh referred me to Dr. Jessica Allen Ching, she's the most amazing plastic surgeon I've ever met. Dr. Ching was incredibly positive; during our first visit. She went over details about using a titanium mesh as part of my reconstruction. She explained with the titanium mesh there was a low risk of infection; if I remember correctly, the risk of infection is < 1%, she also explained the mesh allows for tissues and calcium to build naturally, this made me feel comfortable and at peace. I honestly believe Dr. Ching was a gift from God to complete what needed to be done so I move forward with my life.

Surgery date was set for June 4, 2018; Dr. Hoh would be assisting in the surgery. I felt relieved knowing my two God given doctors were going to work together during my reconstruction surgery.

April 6, 2018 came; it was time for me to return to work, because my medical leave had expired. I had great expectations and decided to return to work. **"Team Belleview"** was waiting for me; I felt I needed to do this. This moment was short lived; It lasted 24 days and on April 30, 2018, I went again on leave because the noise level and work related stress was producing pressure in my head and causing headaches, the doctor determined I needed to rest and prepare for the titanium mesh Cranioplasty on June 4, 2018.

June 4, 2018 arrived! I was so excited and nervous at the same time. The Lord gave me a scripture and promise. **Deuteronomy 28:6** – "You will be blessed when you come in and blessed when you go out.

All I needed is this one verse from God and that's enough for me.

I read it! I believed it! I considered it done!

I'm taking a leap of faith and putting the past behind me. When surgery time got there, I was asked are you ready. My response was yes because, I'm blessed going in and blessed coming out; the anesthesiologist responded," Well there you go.

Jorge asked Dr. Ching if she's going to shave my head; I was relieved when she said no, she would wash my hair, but it wasn't necessary to shave my head. Then, Jorge asked if I would have drain tubes on the incision. She said no because with drain tubes there could be a risk of infection.

Dr. Ching was eliminating all possibilities for infection; that made me feel at peace.

The surgery was a success, no drain tubes were used, and I wasn't placed on Keppra as a preventative for seizures. Dr. Ching felt it wasn't necessary because I've never had seizures. I felt great! No depression, no crying. Recovery went quicker than I expected. Before I knew it; I was being discharged and sent home.

Walking on Beach Sand

July 7, 2018 was the most amazing day of my life!

My youngest son got married!

Joshua and Nichole decided on a beach wedding, with immediate family attending. Jorge did the wedding ceremony. I wanted to be able to walk with Joshua, the day of his wedding. All those therapy sessions; practicing walking, standing on an inclined foam, and standing on soft and hard surfaces. I worked hard at therapy for this moment here.

I lived **Philippians 4:13** – "I can do all things through Christ which strengtheneth me" (KJV). God used my therapist to strengthen me with courage to be able to walk on the beach. Thank you isn't enough. My therapist did an exceptional job at preparing me for this moment.

The moment arrived and I was beyond words. I remember Joshua telling me "Lady" thank you.

I responded, "Baby boy don't thank me; thank God. He's the reason I'm here, God brought me back. Here I am proving to you his Word is true. I'm living Philippians 4:13.

THE AWAKENING

There came a point that I started to spiritually awaken. I began taking back the woman I am in Christ. The pages that follow is a product of that spiritual awakening. I'm so blessed to be alive and to be able to share this with you.

My AVM Daily Scriptures

I put together these scriptures and thoughts as I began my AVM recovery process. I read these every day to remind myself; with God all things are possible!

> **John 9:3 "Neither this man nor his parents sinned," said Jesus, "but this happened so that the works of God might be displayed in him. (NIV)**

> **My Thoughts:**

I didn't do anything wrong to cause the AVM, I suffered an AVM rupture; problem, mountain, adversity, obstacle, call it what you want, so that works of God would be displayed in me.

> **John 10:10 (NIV): The thief comes only to steal and kill and destroy; I have come that they may have life and have it to the full.**

My Thoughts:

Jesus died so that I have and live an abundant life full of his blessings and promises. The choice is mine. I choose not to let anything bring me down, therefore I choose Christ. I choose life!

Jeremiah 33:6 (NIV): "'Nevertheless, I will bring health and healing to it; I will heal my people and will let them enjoy abundant peace and security.

My Thoughts:

God wants me healed. God wants me whole and lacking nothing.

Psalm 103:1–5 (NIV):

- Praise the Lord, my soul; all my inmost being, praise his holy name. 2 Praise the Lord, my soul, and forget not all his benefits 3 who forgives all your sins and heals all your diseases, 4 who redeems your life from the pit and crowns you with love and compassion, 5 who satisfies your desires with good things so that your youth is renewed like the eagle's.

My Thoughts:

Praise the Lord because he's good and wants the best for me. I'm being renewed like the eagle. God wants me whole, well, complete and lacking nothing.

Deuteronomy 28:6 (NIV): You will be blessed when you come in and blessed when you go out.

My Thoughts:

It's God's will for me to be "blessed" therefore I'm BLESSED no matter what I go through.

Hebrews 11:1–3 (NIV): Now faith is confidence in what we hope for and assurance about what we do not see. 2 This is what the ancients were commended for.

3 By faith we understand that the universe was formed at God's command, so that what is seen was not made out of what was visible.

My Thoughts:

Faith is I need to see myself how God sees me; healed, "complete and restored".

I need to call the things that are not as though they were, I need to begin thanking God for my healing or restoration and see myself "healed and restored".

Psalm 27:14 (NIV): Wait for the Lord; be strong and take heart and wait for the Lord.

My Thoughts:

Patience! No need to rush! Wait on the Lord! Patience!

Deuteronomy 30:19 - 20 (NIV): 19 This day I call the heavens and the earth as witnesses against you that I have set before you life and death, blessings, and curses. Now choose life, so that you and your children may live

20 and that you may love the Lord your God, listen to his voice, and hold fast to him. For the Lord is your life, and he will give you many years in the land he swore to give to your fathers, Abraham, Isaac, and Jacob.

My Thoughts:

I choose life. I choose blessing; therefore, I shall live to witness his promises and glory.

Mark 11:23–24 (NIV): "I tell you, if anyone says to this mountain, 'Go, throw yourself into the sea,' and does not doubt in their heart but believes that what they say will happen, it will be done for them. 24 Therefore I tell you, whatever you ask for in prayer, believe that you have received it, and it will be yours.

My Thoughts:

Don't doubt!

Believe!

Believe His word and promises!

I believe I received my healing the day I prayed.

All I have left to do is thank him for my healing.

Isaiah 41:10 (NIV): "So do not fear, for I am with you; do not be dismayed, for I am your God. I will strengthen you and help you; I will uphold you with my righteous right hand".

My Thoughts:

The Lord is with me every step of my recovery process. He is my strength.

Deuteronomy 7:15 (NIV): "The Lord will keep you free from every disease. He will not inflict on you the horrible diseases you knew in Egypt.

My Thoughts:

The Lord heals me. It's His will I recover.

John 10:10 (NIV): "The thief comes only to steal and kill and destroy; I have come that they may have life and have it to the full.

My Thoughts:

Satan tried to destroy/kill me, but God in his infinite mercy brought me back!

I will live a full life in Christ Jesus our Lord!

MY POST AVM POSITIVE STATEMENTS:

As I began recovering; I wrote these statements to remind myself of who I am in Christ Jesus. I read these every day. Through my recovery I've learned it's about renewing the mind with the word. Sometimes we need to change our thoughts and re-wire our brains.

I'm a survivor of an AVM rupture

    I'm alive to witness the glory of God

    I've embraced who I am

    This is me

    I've accepted and gotten comfortable with my current disability

    I understand I'm not permanently disabled

    I'm a work in progress

    The Lord is my strength.

    I'm the daughter of a king

    I'm blessed

    I'm an overcomer

    I am more than a conqueror

    I'm not giving up

    I'll keep pressing forward

Beginning with the End in Mind

Today is August 30, 2019. It has been 2 years 4 months and 24 days since my AVM ruptured on April 6, 2017. I've come a long way in my recovery process.

I used to walk short distances without using a cane and with close by supervision for safety.

I've taken a bold step recently; I walk short distances without a cane and without supervision. I've become independent; by smoothing the bed sheets and making the bed every morning. I'm able to use the bathroom without assistance. I help Jorge by cooking with him, and washing the dishes using my right hand. My cognitive abilities have made progress too. I'm more focused during writing and my thought pattern flows smoothly. During my writing I'm sensing God's purpose.

God has given me the desire to visit churches and share my AVM journey.

I put together a PowerPoint presentation to use during my testimony. Already wrote a letter to send pastors of local churches; expressing my desire to share my AVM journey with their congregation.

My husband always says he read the end of the Bible and it says we win.

Revelations12:11

"They triumphed over him by the blood of the Lamb and by the word of their testimony; they did not love their lives so much as to shrink from death. (NIV)

Every time I hear him say this I rejoice; because that's enough for me.

-This part of the book is called "Beginning with the end in mind". Everyone needs to understand it doesn't matter how difficult the circumstances are. God's word says we win!

I'm committed to keep pressing forward because God's word never returns void or empty, it accomplishes what it was sent to do. In the end I know I'm a winner and only God matters to me. You're probably thinking my circumstances are the worst. I say make the best of it. The Bible says you win and if you think of it; you're already a winner if you made it this far amid chaos.

The Eagle in Me

Isaiah 40:31 (NIV): "but those who hope in the Lord will renew their strength. They will soar on wings like eagles; they will run and not grow weary; they will walk and not be faint.

For the longest time this has been one of my favorite scripture. I've always been fascinated by the eagle.

After my AVM, I'm going through a transformation process. I'm transitioning from being afflicted (welcoming the pity party mentality, welcoming negativity, and allowing fear to overcome my daily thoughts, and letting my emotions get the best of me) to becoming a soaring eagle. I praise God because He kept me during my affliction, and he has given me the most amazing husband, he's been by my side every step of my recovery process. When I've needed a nurse, Jorge has been there. He's been my psychologist, counselor, therapist, praise the awesome God I serve! He's given me more than what I asked for! There's not a day that goes by that I don't think about God, my faith, and what He means to me. I'm left speechless, His grace touched me. I could've gone to eternity, but the Lord gave me the opportunity to come back and recover. I've been moved by mercy and given unmerited favor. I say this because I know that some people haven't made it through an AVM rupture and died. As the days go by; I spend time reading scriptures and meditate on his promises. This has restored me, I've been strengthened in the Word, and have taken my life back. I completely lost sight of who I am in Christ Jesus. God's mercy endures forever! What more could this girl ask for! A palace! (Just kidding) my life belongs to the Lord.

I've been reading about the eagle.

The eagle is a fascinating bird.

There's a story that's circulating through the web about the eagle. I've used it to compare my AVM recovery process. So, the story goes....

The eagle has a lifespan of approximately 70 years.

At age 40 the eagle goes through a process of change. Its beak gets brittle, and its talons get soft and weak with age. This makes it difficult for the eagle to hunt and eat. Eventually, it will starve! Its feathers grow thick and heavy sticking to the chest and wings, impairing flight. My process of change began at age 52. I could've sat in a corner drowning in pain and sorrow. Instead of drowning, I like the eagle, chose the nest on the mountain top. I chose the process of change.

My choice was going through painful therapy, picking up the word, meditating on His promises, and getting my life back. The eagle goes to its nest on the mountain top and has two choices.

One: to do nothing, sit, starve, and face death.

Two: to make the choice of going through a painful process of renewal at age 40. Guess what's the eagle's choice? It chooses a painful process of renewal.

The renewal processes the eagle endures last 150 days. My renewal process is still going, but praise God I've come a long way! Going on 4 years of recovery. Surprisingly, in the past 8 months, my improvement is happening quickly!

Like the eagle I had to make a choice.

If I sat and did nothing most likely I would've been dependent on pain pills. Been alive; but spiritually dead. My recovery would've been a longer process and I wouldn't have seen the progress that I've made.

First, the eagle knocks off the beak by beating it against a rock until it breaks off. I had to work hard at therapy, I'm not going to deny it; at times, the pain was enough to cry, but like the eagle in the story keeps pressing forward with the process of change. I kept doing therapy and resting after each session. I continued reading scriptures on healing and strength.

The eagle waits until the new beak grows back, after the new beak grows, it pulls off the talons because they've become weak and they're no longer useful for capturing their prey. It plucks out its feathers so new feathers grow enabling better flight. Through therapy I corrected my gait and walking. Now I stand taller and walk straight. Every day therapy hurt but I saw the benefit gained from therapy; I kept going back for more "torture".

I made a choice to go through a process of renewal. It doesn't matter what you're going through. It's all about choice. The eagle has a choice, I have a choice, and you have a choice.

So, let's pick up the Bible and begin focusing on God's blessings and promises. Let's keep telling ourselves that this is a temporary process of change and that when we're finished; we'll be renewed like the eagle. We'll be stronger and more prepared for the next battle.

We're gladiators for Christ!

The more I think about my recovery; I realize through painful physical therapy sessions; I can walk without a Cane short distances and I can move my arm.

Through physical therapy I was able to take off my brace (AFO); now I'm using Under Armour basketball sneakers, because the high tops provide ankle support. Through hard work at therapy I'm able to push my stroke arm forward and pull it back; I can bring my wrist up and down. Every time I endure pain I think about the eagle; I know it's a matter of time and I'll be restored.

I think of Paul's letter to the Philippians. **My favorite verse Philippians 4:13 - I can do all things through Christ who strengthens me!**

I know, the Lord is my strength!

If you're curious about the eagle story...

Here's a link to the eagle story:
www.mailsandforwards.com/eagle-rebirth-process

Planting the seed

When life is going great; we place God in this closet and forget about planting the seed of the word in our minds. We barely try to fellowship with Him because our life is wonderful; we don't need him. We tend to get captured by the cares of this world. When the process comes; we want to pull God out of the closet and suddenly, He's our priority. We're ready to reap.

Wait a minute! You can't reap what you didn't sow!

Our pastor Victorio Garcia-Barbon said once during a message; the sower doesn't plant the seed in the middle of a hurricane because it's pointless, all will be lost. You plant the seed when the weather is favorable; this way with attention and care your seed will germinate and your plant will sprout. As the plant grows stronger you take out the weeds so it can grow and eventually produce fruit. Our life is the same; you plant the word in your mind when all is favorable.

The word germinates and you continue to grow by reading more word. You weed out weaknesses and doubt with the word.

When the hurricane comes you reap what you sowed! You reap the benefits of the word. That's what happened to me through my AVM recovery.

My husband and I were diligent in sowing the word, not in the middle of chaos, but when the season was favorable, when the business was booming, and we had a net worth of 1.5 million. When the market crashed, and recession hit. The word carried us through.

When the unexpected AVM hit; it was the word that carried us through.

Stop living like Jesus disappeared at the cross. He died, descended, ascended, sits at the right hand of God and the Bible says he lives forever.

Let's start living like we serve a live God and stop selling ourselves short. Jesus paid the price once. We need to be diligent and sow the seed.

Sink or Walk on Water

I never imagined I'd travel a painful recovery road; but I did. We go through life imagining there's not going to be trials and tribulations; trust me, at times, we all have our share. Life isn't perfect. So, when I faced this painful road; it made me realize I have a choice; I have the choice to sink or walk on water.

My AVM left me thinking about the Apostle Peter and how he walked on water. He was doing great; until he lost focus. His consequence was to begin to sink.

Peter began to sink because he took his eyes off Jesus. Who is Jesus? What does Jesus represent?

John 1:1 (NIV): In the beginning was the Word, and the Word was with God, and the Word was God.

Peter put his focus on the storm that was building around him. Jesus asked him, why did you doubt?

At the beginning of my recovery, I too began to put my focus on the boisterous storm (my AVM); therefore, I began to sink like Peter.

This made me realize that my life depended on the Word. I reached a point that I let the fear of death overwhelm me. I had to make a choice, do I begin to sink like Peter did or do I pick up the word and walk on water? I didn't want to sink because my life depended on it.

My choice was to walk on water. I chose to dwell in the word. Every day is a new beginning for me, and I press forward. With Christ my future is amazing. My past is ugly and tears me down; I don't want to dwell in it too long, but long enough to remind me where I came from. I have a new resurrected life in Christ. He sustains me and gives me strength to keep pressing forward; His word says I'm an overcomer and I'm convinced I am. Don't need anyone to remind or tell me. My question to you is: Are you going to sink or walk on water?

"Love her like Christ loves the church"

These are the words that my husband heard, at the beginning of my AVM recovery. He heard your love will lift her up and that's what Jorge did.

Jorge loved me the way 1 Corinthians 13 describes it. When I had nothing to offer; Jorge loved me like Christ loved the church. I'm talking about the purest form of love where you aren't expecting anything in return. I think it's called companionship. We enjoyed conversations about the word and God's promises. This was the biggest blessing I could receive! My lifelong partner was by my side; he wasn't focused on his needs. He put all on hold to love me like Christ loves the church. This kind of love is exactly what I needed! It lifted me and brought me back to the woman I am in Christ. This kind of love removed all my fears and brought down all the walls I kept putting up.

2 Corinthians 10:4 (NIV): "The weapons we fight with are not the weapons of the world. On the contrary, they have divine power to demolish strongholds".

In the early days of our marriage Jorge was extremely successful. He treated me like a queen, if he could've given me the world, he would have. When God called Jorge to preach; I made the choice to work so he could do what God called him to do. See to me God comes first, and this wife would do whatever she could so that the gospel is preached.

I worked and Jorge preached. When the AVM happened, I needed care 24/7. Jorge made the choice to become my round the clock caregiver. He chose not to go to work and provide me with the best care possible. I admire my husband's choice!

Every Sunday I sit in church hearing the message. I'm left speechless when I see the product of God. God took a man that was a disaster, forgave him, cleansed him of his habit, and built him up to speak his word. Cocaine was Jorge's stronghold and now it's a shadow of his past. The Bible says you reap what you sow, all the care and attention I gave to make sure my husband could fulfill his calling. I've had the blessings come back to me in ways I never imagined. I'm well taken care of and with my disability benefits and retirement pension; we're blessed.

That's more than enough because the gospel is still preached. We haven't lost sight of the calling. God still comes first; we've hit a Valley and are working our way up to the peak. I'm convinced that God always provides, and He has a purpose for everything. His purpose for Jorge and I will be fulfilled no matter what.

ONE IN A MILLION

I went through life not knowing I was a ticking bomb; any minute that bomb would go off. It wasn't anyone's fault. It certainly wasn't my parent's fault, it wasn't anything my husband and sons did, or anything I did. I was born defective and went through life undiagnosed.

The cardiovascular system in my brain didn't develop properly, and it grew into a tangle of veins. The tangle grew so large; it looked like a giant spider web. The years kept passing, until the time pre-determined by God to allow the ticking Bomb to blow. I understand God has a perfect time and plan for everything.

My husband and I weren't babies in the faith. We had reached spiritual maturity and spiritually fed on solid food and there wasn't a need for milk. I strongly believe had my AVM burst sooner we would've lost our faith.

My husband spoke faith words to me and ignored my insanity. I was embarking on an emotional roller coaster and all he could do is quote scriptures; not just any scripture but the words I needed to hear. Every obstacle that arose, my husband, pointed to the word. I don't know what I would've done without him!

Jorge is the one who led me to Christ. It's because of the miracle God did with Jorge; I received Jesus as my savior. To this day, Jorge still leads me to Christ.

The Heart of a Champion

Most of us live busy lives; we get caught up with; family, friends, work, chores, etc. At times, we think we're doing God a favor, by going to church on Sundays.

We have an example of a champion in the Bible. "David". David defeated Goliath.

1 Samuel 17:49–51 (NIV): "Reaching into his bag and taking out a stone, he slung it and struck the Philistine on the forehead. The stone sank into his forehead, and he fell face down on the ground.

50 So David triumphed over the Philistine with a sling and a stone; without a sword in his hand he struck down the Philistine and killed him.

51 David ran and stood over him. He took hold of the Philistine's sword and drew it from the sheath. After he killed him, he cut off his head with the sword. When the Philistines saw that their hero was dead, they turned and ran.

As believers we need to adopt the mindset of a champion.

Imagine how successful our lives would be if we change our mentality and dedicate at least an hour of our day to reading the gospel and meditate in His word. We'd be strong enough to overcome any valley we go through. We'd be elite champions.

Revelation 3:5–6 (NIV): "The one who is victorious will, like them, be dressed in white. I will never blot out the name of that person from the book of life but will acknowledge that name before my Father and his angels. 6 Whoever has ears, let them hear what the Spirit says to the churches.

To be an overcomer requires time; time invested in the word to prepare oneself for battle; just like the aspiring boxer trains and conditions their body three hours a day. We need to train and condition our minds every day.

How do we do that?

Romans 12:2 (NIV): "Do not conform to the pattern of this world but be transformed by the renewing of your mind. Then you will be able to test and approve what God's will is—his good, pleasing and perfect will".

The Apostle Paul knew that our greatest battle is our minds; that's why he instructed us to renew our minds.

How do we do that?

Simple; by setting a schedule and spending time renewing our thought process, with God's word.

Every car or piece of equipment has an owner's manual. In it are instructions teaching us how to properly operate it; and how to give it proper care.

We're the same. How're we going to live the way God intended us to, if we never pick up our owner's manual (The Bible)? You're probably thinking I don't have time for that.

Here's food for thought:

block out on your schedule 15 minutes every day; work your way up to an hour a day. If you come across a day where it's impossible to set aside 15 minutes of your day; don't give up and keep trying.

You have the heart of a champion, an elite champion!

Proverbs 3:7-8 (NIV)

7 "Do not be wise in your own eyes; fear the Lord and shun evil. 8 This will bring health to your body and nourishment to your bones.

You can do this!

Go win Champ!

The Preacher's Kids

The purpose of this section isn't to bash the preacher and his kids. It's to enlighten your understanding with a genuine and constructive outlook; so, we learn to look at the preacher's kids with love, understanding, compassion, and mercy. I have admiration, sympathy, and consideration for a clergyman or clergywoman with a family; particularly when having the responsibility to raise kids.

Parenthood is a continuing learning experience. It's a fact that nobody's perfect; as parents we have good intentions and want the best for our children. We want to shelter them from the world, and in the process; we lose sight they're human beings, with the capability of making mistakes, just like we do.

My mind was consumed when I saw what my husband and sons had to go through because of my AVM.

Proverbs 22:6 (NIV): "Start children off on the way they should go, and even when they are old, they will not turn from it".

The seed of the word has been implanted in them. We need to trust God in His predetermined time; the seed will sprout and bear fruit, fruit that yields a great return.

My Advice

Trust God: speak words of life to your child and start at an early age. If your child is a teen or young adult; don't let that stop you from speaking words of life to them, there's always a commencement. Begin today and keep going! I began by having mine memorize **Philippians 4:13**.

The Power of the Tongue

Have you caught yourself saying, **"the preacher's kids are the worst"?** Stop it! Stop it right now!

Proverbs 15:4 (KJV 1900): A wholesome tongue is a tree of life: But perverseness therein is a breach in the spirit.

The preacher and his kids don't need any favors, especially when nothing wholesome is coming out of your mouth. Pay attention to your words and ask yourself; do I say comments that produce life? With my words do I build up or tear down?

To avoid unwholesome talk; when my boys reached their teenage years, I kept their struggles to myself and prayed for them. Nowadays, I share their struggles as a testimony.

I'm going to give you the same advice I'd tell my students" **if you can't say anything nice; it's best you don't say anything at all".**

Feelings

Like any human being the preacher's kids have feelings. They feel "The Mission" is placed above their needs. At times, they feel all eyes are on them waiting to be put under the scope.

The pastor's kids have learned to walk by faith and not by sight, but at times, it really feels like they're placed in tough situations.

My sons faced the possibility they'd lose me during brain surgery. One-minute life was great; the next minute their world was turned upside down. I was facing brain surgery with the possibility of not making it. If I chose no surgery there's a great risk of not surviving my next rupture. If we think about it; a diamond isn't made until it's put under pressure. I was entering the pressure zone and my diamonds in the rough were forced to face intense pressure!

They faced, hurt, pain, and the uncertainty I would make it. It's enough to cause anyone to default their faith; but my boys had their father as a godly role model to show them what we do amid adversity. **We focus on the Word and above all things; we believe God.**

Certain people and not all people are called to preach, don't expect the preacher's kids to carry it on. We need to understand that the calling to ministry is not for everybody, including the preacher's kids. Mine aren't preachers but they love God and the miracle He did in me. Two are pursuing computer science degrees; the baby of the house chose to be a commercial truck driver. He got his CDL and is happy driving trucks.

The preacher's kids want to be treated like normal kids; expecting great things but allow room for them to make mistakes and failures.

Some have suffered deception at a young age; when they see their parents betrayed by the people they've whole-heartedly helped. This caused them to put up a wall and want nothing to do with the people around their parents; even if it's people in ministry.

Bottom line we have a great responsibility. If we're believers; we need to be a part of the solution and not the problem.

The preacher's kids need our support, not our judgment. Like the singer TobyMac sings "Speak Life" to the preacher's kids. Let's build them up and strengthen them.

John 6:63 (NIV): "The Spirit gives life; the flesh counts for nothing. The words I have spoken to you—they are full of the Spirit and life".

Hit the Mountain

Matthew 17:19–20 (NIV): "Then the disciples came to Jesus in private and asked, "Why couldn't we drive it out?"

20 He replied, "Because you have so little faith. Truly I tell you, if you have faith as small as a mustard seed, you can say to this mountain, 'Move from here to there,' and it will move. Nothing will be impossible for you."

I believe His word is true!

I believe I'm a mountain moving child of the King!

While sleeping the other night; in the background I kept hearing our pastor Victorio Garcia Barbon's voice repeating. "You hit the mountain with the Word. I also heard; you hit the mountain with the word until you see results".

next morning, I prayed. I ordered my brain to rewire with healthy and perfect connections. Ordered my stroke side to restore itself and become fully functioning. Quoted Isaiah 53:5. Then thought; I need to do something. Actions speak louder than words! I'm committed to keep repeating this every day until I see results! It was the birth of Re-wiring My Brain part! I stored it on my phone and read & meditate on what I wrote every day.

<u>Re-wiring my brain</u>

There comes a point in our lives we realize; we can't continue in the same path we've traveled all these years. The AVM brought suffering, hurt, pain, and negative thoughts. Kirk Franklin's song **_"This is it"_** says I can't be here next year giving you these same tears. I refuse to drown in sorrow and know my Lord loves me and wants me whole. Through reading the scriptures; our pastor from south Florida message on the law of association. My husband's messages on Sundays about the mind; renewing the mind with the word. Not letting your brain go way out there in the thought process; instead, bring all thoughts captive to Christ. Don't let your mind control you; you control it by submitting your thinking to the Word. It took me a while; I realized my thought process needed to change and take a negative to a positive. Don't want to be what I think if it's going to be negative.

My inheritance comes from Abraham.

Romans 4:17 (KJV 1900): As it is written, I have made thee a father of many nations, before him whom he believed, even God, who quickeneth the dead, and calleth those things which be not as though they were.

Avoid negative talk.

Proverbs 18:21 (KJV 1900): Death and life are in the power of the tongue:

And they that love it shall eat the fruit thereof.

Work on the brain.

verbs 23:7 (KJV): For as he(man) thinketh in his heart(mind) so is he (man):

How do you covert a negative to a positive?

By speaking positive declarations

Here's mine; based on my AVM recovery needs and health needs; feel free to modify them or write your own, according to your needs. I began thanking the Lord, because every miracle Jesus did, first He thanked the father. I'm expecting a miracle, I'd like to begin by saying…

Lord thank you:

I'm healed

My left arm is working perfectly.

I can grab a cup of water; lift it, and bring it to my mouth, so I can take a drink.

I'm able to fold clothes perfectly with both hands.

I stand and walk balanced on both feet.

I'm able to walk around without the need of supervision

My hamstring is strong and restored.

My Brain is balanced, and my cognitive abilities are complete.

Peripheral vision is restored.

I'm energetic, joyful, and healthy.

I'm perfectly made.

The Lord opens the windows of heaven and pours out blessings in abundance.

I have a constant overflow of blessings.

My titanium mesh is perfectly in place with good and healthy tissues building on it.

I trust you Lord with everything, family, finances, health, book writing, and book publishing.

<u>GRACE</u>

Jorge's parents had been attending Church of the Nazarene's Spanish service; in Miami and their pastor married us. When God delivered Jorge from drugs and alcohol this is the church Jorge went back to because his parents were members there.

August of 1989, my life changed. Seeing the change in Jorge when he became a born-again Christian, this led me to become a born-again believer. We were introduced to traditions and rudiments of men. Coming from a catholic upbringing; mixed with a little Santeria, I began to question everything.

There came a point when rudiments led to these counseling sessions. In these sessions we were told to close our eyes, meditate, and see if God would reveal a sin in our past that's hindering our present life; an open door that gives Satan territory over our life. Everything was about a sin in the past and giving Satan territory. Satan's the destroyer and he'll come in and take over if you give him territory. These counseling sessions became too personal; at some point I was asked if I had thoughts of wanting to abort one of my boys during pregnancy. I responded I love my boys and all my pregnancies were planned. Still, I was told the thought of wanting to abort was an open door and it would give Satan territory over my life and the life of my children "they were at risk from being attacked by the devil".

As the sessions continued, they got more extreme and private. They had me call my mother and asked her if she at some point thought of aborting me. All this was considered an open door for Satan. My poor mother responded, daughter I love you, I wanted to have you, rest assured that thought never crossed my mind.

Sunday, August 18,1991, after church service, the pastor approached me and said he wanted me to meet someone. I followed him to the ministry kitchen, and he introduced me to a female guest from their associate church in Argentina. When the woman came to hug me something in my spirit rejected it and I quickly thought "don't let her hug you", so I took a step back and extended my hand not to be rude, she grabbed my hand and shook it. She told me she had been praying for me and wanted to have a counseling session with me, that day. I excused myself and said I couldn't stay because I had to go to the hospital to do pre-op labs, because I was scheduled for a c-section Monday morning at 5am. I got in the car and Jorge noticed my countenance. He asks what's wrong? I told him about the woman and what happened. I told Jorge it's something I can't explain but, in my spirit, I feel this isn't of God and don't want to go through with this counseling session, today. Jorge asked are you sure, I'm convinced that this isn't of God and it's what God wants me to do. Jorge said well do what God wants you to do and don't go to counseling.

After the hospital pre-op I went to my mother's house to do my pedicure.

Jorge calls me and tells me the pastor was paging him nonstop that I should call him and explain my experience.

I call the pastor and explained to him my surgery's early in the morning, and needed to be calm and rested. He kept insisting I had to go to counseling.

Seeing his persistence, I told him, I felt this wasn't from God and felt I didn't have to go through this type of counseling. He was offended and said he was the pastor and insisted I go through with counseling. Then I said to him, pastor I'm not coming to the counseling session.

He was disappointed and told me I was in rebellion and during the c-section Satan could attempt to take my baby's life, because I'd given Satan territory by refusing counseling. I responded I'm sorry you feel that way, but I don't believe God would allow my son to die because a decision I made. All I could think of is the verse where Jesus said let the children come to me for theirs is the kingdom of heaven, and responded to him, my son that's about to be born is innocent; we have nothing more to talk about and I hung up the phone.

A little while after hanging up; the phone rings and it was my aunt Maria. She told me she was calling because God told her to tell me not to worry about the surgery because her church La Cathedral del Pueblo, were going to be praying for me and the baby. She said God has you and the baby in his hands, he is in control of everything, don't you worry about a thing, the baby is going to be healthy and fine. I started crying and thanked her; and told her about my experience with the pastor for being honest and speaking truth. She said Wow I didn't know, but don't you worry about this, God is in control of everything.

she said goodbye and hung up the phone. The power of words! Words can build up or tear down; that day the pastor's words did enough damage to last a lifetime, it left me completely devastated.

My mother noticed my tears and asked daughter what's wrong? When I told her, she said that man's an animal he should be more considerate with you knowing that you're pregnant.

The day of delivery came I was so nervous because I kept thinking of the pastor's words, when time came for my epidural, I yelled at the anesthesiologist because the epidural hurt(epidural always hurts nothing new), he said I was being difficult. I fired back I wouldn't be so difficult if he knew how to do his job! He said if I kept it up, he would put me under general anesthesia, and I would miss seeing my baby boy being born. This made me angry and I began to argue with him. Just then

Dr. Albert my obstetrician came in and said he wanted a minute alone with me. He reminded me I wasn't a newbie at this; this was child number three. Then he asked if I trusted him; I said yes. Dr. Albert signaled for the anesthesiologist to come in. He said we're going to do this together; he coached me through deep breathing and when he saw I was calm, he told the anesthesiologist I'm going to hold her hands and hold her down to assist with the epidural. They gave me a pillow to hold to assist with the bending forward. On the count of three Dr. Albert held me down, epidural was done perfectly, my baby boy's delivery was underway. Delivery went great there were no complications. My little Joshua was born healthy and perfect.

He looked like me!!

God always has a plan and he takes care of you.

Just when I thought it was over. The pastor shows up at the hospital to visit after the delivery. His wife came with him; she told me maybe there's a misunderstanding, the pastor hadn't expressed himself correctly, maybe the timing wasn't right. He boldly interrupted her and told her they didn't need to apologize, he stood firm and said I was in rebellion and I gave Satan territory and Satan still could take the baby's life.

I said I'm sorry, but I don't agree with you. We have nothing more to talk about and they left.

The days that followed I developed anxiety. I found comfort and strength in His word. His grace surrounded me, and seeing my little Joshua was a healthy baby, I lost the fear and developed trust. Joshua and I were discharged from the hospital.

Something changed after this incident. I refused to go back to church and be put through that again. We read the word and decided to look for a place to fellowship.

We visited a couple of churches, but something was missing. My brother in law was married to the daughter of a church member. When I shared with her what happened, and told her we were looking for a different place to fellowship, she told me I should visit the church La Palabra Revelada. Pastor Victorio and Betty Garcia - Barbon preach a word of grace, she thought I would benefit from their message. We visited a Sunday and received the word of grace, we kept coming back every Sunday for more instruction in the word.

You're wondering What is Grace?

It's the period that began after Jesus ascended to heaven (Acts1:9-12), and the period we live in. The church is called to live by Grace **(see the Epistles of the Apostle Paul).** Jesus was crucified, died, descended, preached to those that were in the bosom of Abraham. He resurrected on the third day; walked the earth and ascended to heaven, he sits at the right of the Father **(see the book of Acts).**

Grace is something simple; yet we make it complicated. It's a gift given freely to all those who receive it and choose to live by it.

There's a misconception that Grace is a ticket to sin; I say it's not, it's a choice and a lifestyle. We go through a continuous cycle of thought renewal. We choose to receive the sacrifice of Jesus Christ.

We choose to obey and live by the word. Grace can't be combined with the law and traditions of men; to do so invalidates the gift we've been given. We have been given a better covenant, based on the sacrifice of Jesus.

Hebrews 8:6–11 (NIV): "But in fact the ministry Jesus has received is as superior to theirs as the covenant of which he is mediator is superior to the old one, since the new covenant is established on better promises.

7 For if there had been nothing wrong with that first covenant, no place would have been sought for another. 8 But God found fault with the people and said: "The days are coming, declares the Lord, when I will make a new covenant with the people of Israel and with the people of Judah. 9 It will not be like the covenant I made with their ancestors when I took them by the hand to lead them out of Egypt because they did not remain faithful to my covenant, and I turned away from them, declares the Lord. 10 This is the covenant I will establish with the people of Israel after that time, declares the Lord.

I will put my laws in their minds
    and write them on their hearts.

I will be their God, and they will be my people. 11 No longer will they teach their neighbor, or say to one another, 'Know the Lord, 'because they will all know me, from the least of them to the greatest.

You need to dispose your mind of excess baggage and traditions of men.

Have you caught yourself thinking "I need to do this because that's how my family did it" or "I need to do this because the preacher said I have to, if I want to become a member". John said it perfectly. **John 4:24(NIV)**- "God is spirit, and his worshipers must worship in the Spirit and in truth." Stop following what everyone does and worship Him or seek Him in spirit and truth.

We have been programmed to follow what everyone does.

To sum it up; traditions and rudiments of men taught me that I was worthless. Everything gave Satan territory. It taught me fear and depleted me of my identity in Christ.

When I visited pastors Victorio and Betty the first time; something changed.

They taught me grace; I received back my identity in Christ and the scales came off. Every Sunday Jorge and I went back for more biblical instruction. It was opening our eyes and we saw the truth in His word. We felt revived, forgiven, and uplifted. Something changed. We went from a negative to a positive. We found a new life in Christ. We liked this new life and wouldn't go back to traditions and rudiments of men. It kept us enslaved and grace broke the chains that kept us bound.

I'm convinced Grace calls us to do what's uncommon/unpopular.

We don't do things because every Christian does it that way. We stand firm on the instructions found in the epistles of the Apostle Paul.

The Law was given to Moses for Israel, it's not for the New Testament Church. In the law we find condemnation, making it impossible to fulfill the law. In Grace we have been justified by Jesus' sacrifice.

1 John 2:1 (NIV): "My dear children, I write this to you so that you will not sin. But if anybody does sin, we have an advocate with the Father—Jesus Christ, the Righteous One.

Jesus fulfilled the law, so we don't have to. Grace is a constant renewal of our mind through the word, and it means having a compromise to live by the Word and believing in the finished work of Jesus Christ. We don't practice sin; but If we fall short, we have an advocate in Christ Jesus our Lord.

Through my recovery Jorge and I had the word. I didn't have a preacher come lay hands on me or pour oil on me. There was no counseling session, and there was no fear of what I've done that gave Satan territory. Simply put, I have a loving husband who shared my faith and quoted God's word. Believed the Word above all circumstances.

Isaiah 55:11 (NIV): "so is my word that goes out from my mouth: It will not return to me empty but will accomplish what I desire and achieve the purpose for which I sent it.

Grace shows us to believe and depend on His word. It takes away Satan's authority. Grace gives us access to the throne based on Jesus' sacrifice.

Grace also taught me to know God and know his word. When the AVM came; I did what the word says. I approached the thrown of Grace with confidence because I knew God hears me and He cares for me.

My Husband Jorge's Reflection About My AVM

My pain and suffering started 30 days before my wife's AVM bursting on April 6, 2017.

One morning; towards the end of February, around eight o'clock, my mother calls, she's asking me to hurry up and go to their house, my father is on the floor and he can't get up or talk.

Immediately, my heart started racing, began crying and told Maria I was afraid of this call, because this was my dream 6 months ago. My wife looked at me bold in the face and said," We're warriors and soldiers of the Gospel, so suck it up and fight because that's what we do".

As I entered my car and began driving to my parent's house; I prayed to my Lord and savior, saying, "Lord please give me strength to face this tragedy." You're a miracle working God. The drive there was peaceful, until the moment I arrived, got out of my car, walked up their entry, and opened their door.

I walk in and find my mother sitting in the family room towards the back of the house. Asked her where's dad? She answered, he's in the hallway.

Seeing him lying on his face; he couldn't move or talk; my heart was torn. I picked him up; and held him on my laps and said, dad it's going to be okay. Asked if he had any pain and he said no. He told me for approximately four hours he kept talking to the Lord while he was on the floor; telling him he didn't want to die. Then he remembered Matthew 7:7-8 (NIV) 7 "Ask and it will be given to you; seek and you will find; knock and the door will be opened to you. 8 For everyone who asks receives; the one who seeks finds; and to the one who knocks, the door will be opened".

After he told me this, the paramedics got there, and took him to the hospital, where they told him he had a TIA. Seven days later they took him to Avante at Ocala rehab for therapy. For twenty-nine days, I went to the rehab; took him clothes and food.

He gets discharged from Avante; I took him home, set up his house for him, hugged him and said, well dad I'm going home to rest and get some sleep.

I kissed him and started walking towards my car and the phone rang. It was my wife calling me from her job to tell me she wasn't feeling well.

She explained she was talking to her team teachers about her students and our kids when they were young and suddenly, she felt something go down her spine and her legs got weak. She felt like she was going to fall. So, I told her I'll meet you at the house.

When I arrived, I walked into the kitchen looked towards the living room and see her lying on the sofa dozing off and ask her; how are you feeling? She said my neck is stiff and I feel dizzy. My thought was maybe her neck was out of alignment and decided to take her back to the urgent care where she had been 30 days before with the same symptoms. At that earlier visit, they told her it was work related stress and gave her medicine, to relieve muscle spasm and sent her home. We walked into the urgent care and explain to them we came here 30 days ago, and we're back because she's feeling worse than last time.

Now it's to the point her neck froze, and she couldn't move it. They told us there's a one- hour wait to see a doctor. We take a seat in the waiting area to wait for a doctor.

Maria was feeling worse and tells me I can't wait long; I feel horrible, please take me to the emergency room at the hospital. We informed the reception area I've decided to take her to Monroe Regional hospital.

We walk out and got in the car; As we're driving out of the urgent care Maria told me to stop the car; she opened the door and she started throwing up. That was enough for me to realize this is more serious than I thought. So, I told her we're going straight to Monroe hospital. We arrived at the hospital went up to the emergency's front desk and explained her symptoms to the nurse and they told me there was a two-hour wait. We take a seat to wait for a doctor. Maria's symptoms were getting worse; she threw up again.

I complained to the nurse about my wife's condition and the nurse replied she was going to talk to the doctor on duty about her.

Thank God, in about fifteen minutes they called us back to see the doctor!

Maria explains to the doctor what happened to her thirty days ago. The doctor told us he was going to talk to the other doctor. About fifteen minutes later he came back and told us that based on what we told him, and this being the second time this has happened, he has decided to do an MRI of her brain. So, they took her back to do the MRI. While waiting at the room, I'm now beginning to worry a little, because they decided to do an MRI, I'm thinking it could be brain related.

The MRI results are in and they show Maria has liquid in her brain possibly blood. The doctor tells me to make sure, he's going to have them repeat the MRI. Imagine! First, my father suferred a TIA and now my wife has fluid in her brain. Confused and torn by the awful news, I stepped out to the lobby to let the family know that Maria has fluid in her brain, possibly blood and they're repeating the MRI.

I call our sons to give them this awful news and they said they'll be on their way. I come back to see Maria and became upset because she wasn't in the room. I complained to the nurse, how can you move my wife from her room without notifying me! The nurse asked me to calm down and redirected me to the room they put her in, I get there to find Maria surrounded by doctors and I hear we're sending her to Shands hospital because she suffered a brain bleed.

`At that moment, I was overwhelmed with emotions. Shocked because of the awful news. I asked them is this something you can take care of here; they said they weren't equipped to take care of this kind of problem. I felt anxiety and with it came fear.

Everything happened so fast, that I didn't have time for anything. One minute they're repeating the MRI and the next minute, they're rushing to get her to Shands hospital.

As they were wheeling her in the transport bed to put her in the ambulance. I got down by her side, and began to say, this isn't fair, you're a good woman, you don't deserve this. Maria interrupted me "stop it! Stop it right now! You have your testimony for God, and I have nothing, this is my testimony for God.

They put her in the ambulance, closed the door and took off.

I was shocked and disoriented to the point I couldn't drive. So, our son Joshua said, "I'll drive you to Shands hospital".

When I arrived at Shands Hospital and walked into her room, Maria said Dr. Hoh was waiting for her outside the entrance with his neuro team and they told her not to worry, he's the best in this field.

Next morning the doctors gave me the bad news, she has a brain AVM. It gets worse when Dr. Corliss tells me this is one of the biggest AVM they've seen. AVMs go from category 1-5 Maria's AVM was almost a four, they were having difficulty getting the insurance's approval for this surgery.

Insurance only approves category 1 – 3 because the risk of death is extremely high on an AVM above a 3. So, they re-evaluated the AVM and rewrote it as a low 3 category and the insurance approved her surgery. On April 7th, they did an angiogram to the brain to try to glue all the arteries in the AVM. At this point I am in shock and locked out. Our sons said I was reiterating everything the doctor said. The truth is I was irate and started questioning my faith.

The possibility of losing the woman of my youth during brain surgery was more than I can endure.

She had been with me through drug addiction. God used her to open my eyes. Maria helped me become the man I am today; she was by my side every step of the way.

Together we became one in Christ, we share the same thoughts, expectations, and dreams. She was the one God used. Maria saw the real me through God's eyes and helped me change.

It was hard to see myself in this situation because we spent years serving families in our church, since I became a believer.

Why did God allow this to happen to her?

Couldn't he spare her from the pain and suffering?

My wife has been a good woman. She loves God. She is kingdom minded and doesn't deserve this.

The angiogram took four hours. Dr. Corliss came in and explained they couldn't get to one of the arteries. I became worried when the doctor told me he couldn't get to one of the arteries to glue it.

I understood that was going to be a higher risk for brain bleed.

The world was caving in on me. The big question… "Lord why her"?

I started searching the internet about AVMs of the brain and discover that most patients after surgery die within 48 hours.

After reading this, my faith was totally crushed and one of my daughters in law is a critical care nurse, she wasn't having much hope for Maria's survival of such massive AVM surgery. I was so broken mentally, physically, and spiritually. To top it off; this happened three days before her birthday.

Our family wanted to celebrate her birthday, and they asked the ICU nurse if we could celebrate it. They said yes and we brought her a cake, balloons, and presents. The craziest things were going through my mind.

Is this going to be her last birthday?

I'm not ready to be alone or to lose her.

Is she going to make it?

As I looked around the room and saw all the sad faces without hope; this didn't make it any better for me, my heart disintegrates, and in my mind, I was saying... Lord why have you abandoned us?

For 28 years all we've done is serve you.

I felt weak, powerless, and hopeless.

April 9, 2017, we were all in her room singing happy birthday and still wondering is this going to be her last birthday. Maria asks me to play her favorite song (Holy Spirit) that is on her phone. This is too much for me to handle, so I gave her phone to one of our family members, to play the song. Maria begins to sing the song, tears started rolling down her cheeks, they sent us out, because her heart rate went up.

Later, after celebrating her birthday Dr. Corliss came in to talk to us about the surgery and the high risk for complication and of course signing the consent paperwork for her surgery. Our family decided that was our decision, and they stepped outside to give us some privacy.

Maria looked at me and said why don't we just go home. I told her I wish I could take your place; this isn't fair you're a great wife, mother, daughter, and woman of God.

Then I explained to her I couldn't take her home knowing that she has an AVM. Knowing it was having small bleeds and taking a chance she could die in her sleep. So, we decided to go through with the surgery, and she gave me all authority to make her life decisions. Feeling so drained and hopeless, without sleep or food for three days.

It was getting late and Maria needed to rest for the surgery, told her I love you, and I'll see you in the morning.

That night I couldn't sleep; all kinds of thoughts were going through my mind… Why her? This isn't fair and certainly not the plan of God. The word of God promises to bless, heal, and prosper us.

All night I was having the battle of my life and making sense of my 28 years of being a Christian, preaching his word and seeing all kinds of miracles. I was faithless, weak, and miserable. This is more than I can handle, with palpitations in my heart, I was deeply sorrowed and thought... Lord, where are you?

April 10, 2017 (surgery day) about eight in the morning, the nurse said they were getting ready to take Maria back to the surgery room.

I told our family let's pray, while praying, I felt weak and hopeless and I continued praying. It was the right thing to do. We finished praying, gave her a kiss and told her, we'll see you soon.

We were all standing at the waiting room hallway when they rolled Maria past us to the surgery room, she looked at me worried and scared, I was deeply sorrowed and worried.

It's now ten in the morning, we've had no updates and we were worried. As I was sitting on the floor outside of the waiting room; a man was passing by, he stopped and looked at me and said, as I walked past you, I felt such anguish coming from you, it caught my attention.

For a minute I realized that the God that seemed silent and nowhere to be seen, sent an angel to my rescue. I began to explain my situation to him. When I was finished, he told me he was a pastor. He asked me if he could pray with my family and me. As he started praying tears were coming out. After he left, I felt relief and guilt.

Still more questions kept going through my mind.

Why Lord have I become so weak?

I knew my family is depending on me for strength, and I wasn't mentally there.

Time kept passing by and now two in the afternoon with no update about Maria's surgery, I was beginning to get worried because they told me it was about a four-hour surgery.

Finally, I saw the chief of staff and asked her to please give us an update about what's going on that nobody has given me an update about the surgery, she told me all she knew is they were still in surgery and couldn't tell me anything else at the moment.

We were worried after six hours of surgery with no information or update. Many things were running through my mind knowing it was a complicated and high-risk surgery.

For the first time in my life I felt powerless, knowing, I always made Maria a promise… if I break it, I'll fix it. I couldn't believe Maria was facing a life-threatening surgery, and I couldn't do anything to fix this.

All I kept thinking about; I was taking care of my father for thirty days after his stroke, and the same day I took my dad home from the rehab, walking out of my parent's house, I got Maria's phone call, saying, she wasn't feeling well.

Now I'm here four days later with my wife in a critical condition.

For a moment I said Lord is this a dream or is this real.

Three more hours went by, it's almost 5 p.m. with no update. Fifteen minutes earlier they rolled a bed down the hallway with somebody deceased and you could hear the wife screaming and crying.

No!

Why did he die?

No Lord no!

This was more than I could handle. Just about five I was standing by the elevator; my heart began to flutter, and I began to feel like something was wrong. Then I began pacing the hallway telling my family something is wrong. When I said that to my mother in law; she thought somebody gave me an update.

Then, I said to her it was a feeling and it troubled me.

I knew something is wrong. About six (an hour later) I went to the ICU door and used the phone by the door and asked is Maria in her room?

Thinking maybe they bypassed us through another section of the hospital. The chief of staff said no she's not out of surgery yet. When I walked out to my wife's parents. My family asked me, is she out of surgery? I said no.

A few minutes later a female doctor from the neurosurgery team was walking towards the waiting room. I walked towards her and she asked if I was Gonzalez family.

I said I'm her husband.

I asked where is Dr. Hoh?

She said he couldn't come out to talk to me.

I asked how's my wife?

She was hesitating to explain to me. There were complications during surgery, she might not see well from her right eye, as she was looking towards the floor. Her shuddering voice and sad look made me think my wife was dying.

We were devastated. I became so anxious and out of my mind. When the ICU doors opened; I ran into the ICU room, where Maria had been for three days. As I'm standing in the room a doctor dressed in black walks in and asked me, what are you doing in here? I responded I'm her husband. He answers please step outside we are going to be busy stabilizing her. They bring her in and park her bed. The doctor looks at Maria and begins to yell MARIA WAKE UP! He shakes her three times and Maria is still nonresponsive.

The doctor calls critical code and asks the other doctor for an intubation kit. That moment was devastating.

My faith was crushed seeing my wife, looking like she was dying before my eyes.

She had purple lips, swollen and ashy face leaning towards her chest.

At that moment, I felt like I was dying and went into shock. I was told I had to leave, because nobody can be in the room under critical code to stabilize the patient. I was thinking, she's dying, and they don't want to tell me the truth. The toughest part is to face the family, especially her parents who are old.

I went out and told the family the doctors said she's critical and they're working to stabilize her.

It was late, I haven't slept or eaten in four days and the family told me it's better to wait to the morning.

I looked at my daughter in law Cassy and saw she didn't have much hope that Maria was going to make it to morning.

We walked outside the hospital; I couldn't breathe. I started running for two blocks nonstop and my son Joshua was chasing me and said dad stop. I stopped, sat down on some steps, and began to cry. I felt desolate, miserable, and abandoned by God.

As I sat that night in the hotel room, I couldn't sleep, thinking the last six years of my life have been hell.

2010 the economy falls and the market crashes.

My main contractor calls me to tell me he's sorry; they lost their main account and they don't have any more work. Through this Maria supported me and assured me that God will never forsake us, and He always provides.

I had to close my business and lay off my employees. I lost my truck, my boat and Maria's beautiful home, I built for her in Crystal River, was deeded back to the bank. We had to move into the church and convert the garage into a pastoral live in quarters. The truth is though I lost everything; I was blessed because I still had the church, my faith and Maria. Now the only thing I had left and worth living for; is fighting for her life.

The truth is I just wanted to crawl in a hole and die.

On April 11 we were at the hotel room waiting for the doctors to give us updates.

That afternoon my son Joshua had to go home because he had to work. He called me when he left and said dad, I got to see mom, I'm going to stop by the hospital on the way home. I said, let me know how you see her.

My son called and told me dad don't come see her it's a horrible site. Her head is deformed the swelling is so bad, her eyes are sticking out of her head. Joshua was so overwhelmed, he and his wife Nichole, suggested for me to stay at the hotel until the swelling went down and the doctors would update me daily because she looked terrible, this is too much for you to handle. So, I agreed.

April 12 around three in the morning, the ICU doctor called wanting approval to put a probe into her brain to monitor the swelling. I asked why and he said if the swelling gets bad, she can have permanent brain damage. I gave him the approval.

An hour later the doctor called me and said the probe was successful. I spent four days in the hotel praying and reconnecting with my faith, especially when I would ask the question. When is my wife going to wake up? The answer would always be, we don't know.

April 14 at ten in the morning, I walked into ICU to see Maria. The swelling was gone, but I was devastated to see she was totally intubated, on life support and hoses going into her body everywhere, so many bags of drugs, IVs, and a monitor on her head to detect if she's having a seizure.

This sight of her condition was more than I can handle. I waited all day to see the doctors in charge to ask them the question. Is she going to make it? The answer… we don't know.

I realized that science couldn't do anymore for her; it's all about waiting to see. So, I went back home.

On April 16 around two in the morning, I got on my knees, cried out to God, groaning from my spirit man, telling God that I wasn't asking him to do anything, but I wanted Him to fulfill his word.

The one I've been preaching for years; witnessing miracles and healings. I said Lord; two good things have happened in my life. The first one; your son Jesus Christ coming into my life. The second one; Maria; which I know you put in my life to restore me from my past of drugs and alcohol.

Please don't take her away from me.

I believe in the power of the resurrection and just as you lifted Lazarus; you can lift maria and I'll witness the power of the resurrection for the rest of the days you give me on earth.

I felt peace as I felt the presence of God.

He reminded me **of Isaiah 55:11(NIV) - so is my word that goes out from my mouth:**

It will not return to me empty,

but will accomplish what I desire

and achieve the purpose for which I sent it.

I knew the great I AM was with me and for me. I had the creator of heaven and earth in my corner. That night I wrote forty healing scriptures and had God's promise that his word never comes back void.

For the next nine days, I sat by her bed side reading all forty scriptures and confessing that she's going to walk, talk and worship God like she used to.

When the nurses would come in; I would tell them according to God's word, she's going to be fine. On the fourteenth day after her surgery they started to reduce the induced coma meds; to see if she would respond and wake up. The following day at two in the morning they called me and said her lungs weren't functioning well and her carbon monoxide was going up and asked me if I would give them permission to do a tracheotomy.

I thought she has been through enough pain and suffering already. That procedure produces scar tissue and problems for the future. The nurse said the situation wasn't life threatening now, but it's getting there. Didn't feel peace about it and told the nurse I was down the road in a hotel to call me if it got critical. I prayed myself to sleep asking the Lord to please strengthen her lungs. Woke up at five in the morning and rushed to the hospital and saw the most beautiful thing.

The answer to my prayer.

Maria was wearing a nebulizer mask and she was off life support.

I asked the nurse what happened? She said last night suddenly her lungs kicked in and started working so they started giving her nebulizer treatments. Her lungs started getting stronger every hour and by the next morning when I came in, she was off the mask and breathing on her own. God had been answering all my prayers. The only thing left was for her to wake up. After a long day of waiting and confessing the word over her. At almost midnight the nurses told me to go home and rest. Went to the hotel, slept, and got up early in the morning. I prayed and said Lord this is the day you have made and I will rejoice in it, and declare that maria will wake up today for your glory and I remembered that Jesus needed to feed five thousand people. He had a little boy with loaves and two fishes and looking up to heaven, he gave thanks and broke them.

That was my revelation from God for her miracle. I realized that Jesus didn't ask God his father to do a miracle; he gave his father thanks for the miracle, which leaves no room of doubt before God.

This morning I was ready to see the power of the resurrection in Maria's life because of the revelation of Isaiah 55:11 and Luke 9:16. So before

I left to the hospital I raised my hands towards heaven and gave thanks to God for her miracle. As I drove to the hospital the anointing of God was so strong, it felt like I was walking on a cloud and no doubt this is the day God has made and I will rejoice in it.

As I was walking to her room, the presence of God was strong. When I walked in the room and looked at her, she looked like an angel sleeping, and putting my hand on her, declared I command you to wake up in the name of Jesus Christ and come out of that coma now. I sat by her bed and waited with great expectancy for her to wake up. Three hours had gone by and it was almost lunch time. I said to the nurse I'm going down to the cafeteria for lunch and she said ok Mr. Gonzalez we have your number.

I got to the cafeteria, bought my lunch and right when I was about to bite into my sandwich my phone rang. It was the nurse saying Mr. Gonzalez your wife has finally woken up from her coma, but we can't understand what she's trying to say with her right hand. I dropped my sandwich and ran up to the room. I got there, as Maria was trying to open her eyes to look around and using sign language saying she loves everyone. At that moment, I was so grateful to God and with no doubt He manifested his glory and the power of the resurrection. Even though, we had some challenges ahead of us, because the stroke she suffered, after the surgery. I knew that the same God that promised me to resurrect Maria, was the same God that was going to restore her for his glory. No matter how big the mountain might be. We'll never give up our faith in God!!

Jesus said in mark 11:22-24(NIV)

22 "Have faith in God," Jesus answered.

23 "Truly[a] I tell you, if anyone says to this mountain, 'Go, throw yourself into the sea,' and does not doubt in their heart but believes that what they say will happen, it will be done for them.

24 Therefore I tell you, whatever you ask for in prayer, believe that you have received it, and it will be yours.

My daughter-in-Law Cassy's Reflection about my AVM

"Lord if it's you; command me to come to you on the water". So, he said, "Come". And when Peter had come down out of the boat, he walked on the water to go to Jesus. But when he saw that the wind was boisterous, he was afraid and beginning to sink he cried out, saying Lord save me!" Matthew 14:28-30.

We like to think as Christians that we can have faith through any trial. Those life events will never waver or weaken our belief, because after all we have a relationship with the creator of the entire universe. We are held in his hand and nothing can reach us if we are safe in his covering. We like to think that we are exempt from tragedy because we belong to Him.

It's easy to have unshakable faith when life in the "boat" is good. When the seas of our world are calm, and the wind is soft and light. The afternoon of April 6, 2017 my "boat" was thrown into a thrashing angry sea. I received the call that Maria's CT showed blood in her spinal cavity and that she was being rushed to Shands in a critical state. She was diagnosed with an AVM that had burst and was now putting her very life in danger.

As with any crisis in a family, ours banded together. In a matter of hours there we all stood at her bedside with tear filled eyes and heavy hearts.

Praying; for the only thing that could truly save her life, a miracle!

The next day would prove to be one of the biggest tests my faith had ever come up against.

Maria's surgery lasted for ten of the longest hours of my life.

Sitting in that waiting area; surrounded by family, reading the word, and praying every healing scripture over her that came from my spirit man wasn't enough to keep the doubt from slipping into my mind. Looking into the eyes of my husband and children, watching the pain of the situation consumed them I prepared for the worst. As a mother, wife, and Christ follower I repeated to them how through this tragedy God would show us how powerful he was. That we were to be witnesses to a true miracle, but as a critical care nurse I knew that the likelihood of her making it out of this type of surgery alive and fully functional was slim.

Maria's prognosis was poor and knowing what the following months to years held for her if she survived surgery left my faith in a dwindling state. Once she was in recovery, we could see her. The surgeon had warned us that there was massive swelling and that while in surgery she had a significant stroke, which caused damage to her left side. I tried to hold on to even the smallest amount of mustard seed faith I had; that this wouldn't be the end of a woman that I had grown to love so much.

Pulling the curtain back and laying eyes on her in her recovery room my faith was crushed. I started to sink just as Peter had when he took his focus off Christ. The "wind and rain" of this tragedy was too great for me to bear any faith that she could make it through this type of injury let alone make it through the night with her life.

I walked up to her bedside and picked up her small hand trying to hold back a flood of emotions. I wanted to be as strong as I could for my husband, my children, and my family. I leaned in as best I could and kissed her cheek and in that moment something in my spirit broke. How could a woman so Godly, so faithful to God be subjected to this type of pain?

If we truly sit in his hand, how could he have let this happen to her? She was the epitome of a Proverbs 31 woman and yet here she lay fighting for her life. Where was God? Why had he allowed this situation to touch her? Why had not he reached from heaven and intervened before the AVM burst? All I felt as I stood in her recovery room that night was anger.

I felt anger at God; for not stopping this. I was angry at the storm that was now raging around my family.

How would I tell my kids that their grandmother's life was now on the line? How could I remain positive for my husband who was watching his mother fight for her life? The storm was too great, and I felt I was sinking as Peter had done when he took his eyes off Christ. My faith was beaten out of my spirit. The reality of the situation was too loud to be drowned out and I was preparing myself for the worst. As I held her hand for what I thought would be the last time, in my soul I said my goodbyes to a woman that had grown from a mother in law, to a mentor and to my friend.

"Immediately Jesus stretched out his hand and caught him. And said to him, "O you of little faith, why did you doubt"? And when they got into the boat the wind ceased". Matthew 14:31-32.

If I'm being honest, I thought that Maria was going to be present with the Lord that night. I never expected her to wake up and be functional again. Her surgery was so long, and she had such a large complicated stroke that I couldn't see past what my experience as a nurse had shown me over and over again……that patients that fight against odds like the ones that Maria was facing don't have any futures. But God had different odds for Maria.

Each day that passed she woke up more and more. Her journey has been so long but also so full of God's grace. I have watched this woman fight through pain, anxiety, fear, and moments of depression. She has walked through the valley of the shadow of death and come to the other side stronger than I ever thought was imaginable. God has truly shown me his great power through Maria's journey. I have seen with my own eyes miracles that only God could perform.

God not only healed Maria but used this situation to exercise my faith. My faith was weak amid the tragedy because I took my eyes off Christ. I let my flesh and fear consume my mind and that caused me to sink. But just as Christ caught Peter, he caught me as well.

The past 18 months has brought not only healing to Maria but to me as well. I look at her now and I see God's power and healing working inside of her. With each new milestone she reaches I feel my faith being renewed once more. I hear the voice of God asking me why I was one of such little faith. God can use even the worst situation as an outlet for his glory to shine through. This journey with Maria has taught me that even when we see no way out, God has a plan. He has gone before us and prepared a way for us. We need just to have faith as small as a mustard seed and trust him.

Moving Forward from the Disaster

My oldest granddaughter Gloria was affected by my AVM and had a difficult time moving forward.

Gloria put together these statements/thoughts about her feelings after my AVM. We used them to talk about it with the purpose of helping her move past the hurt and pain.

I do this for the Glory of God.

I'm beginning to see the glory of God in me and have come to understand that faith in the kingdom of God was at stake and there was a lot to lose. My family's faith would have been destroyed if I had passed into eternity.

Below is a list of Gloria's statements/thoughts and I've written my responses in Bold. I feel privileged and Blessed to be given the opportunity to survive an AVM; and to be able to help my granddaughter move forward. I'm blessed to be her grandmother; Gloria's a sweet girl and loves the Lord.

Gloria: You're not the same momma that you were before the AVM.

You're right; I'm not the same momma. I was full of hurt and pain after the AVM; but God has brought me back, He's restoring me, and I'm getting stronger. I know I'll recover.

Gloria: I have a hard time looking at pictures of you before the AVM.

Are you thinking of this event like a timeline? Yes. **You're thinking about my life before the AVM and my life after the AVM.** Yes. **I think about that excessively. Don't worry about me, I'm getting stronger every day and I'm recovering, soon I'll look like I did before the AVM. Let's focus on the present, think of how far I've come and the progress I've made.**

Gloria: Why did God allow this to happen to you?

That's a good question, I don't know the answer to that question, and I asked the same question for the longest time. God answered that question for me with this scripture.

John 9:3 - "Neither this man nor his parents sinned," said Jesus, "but this happened so that the works of God might be displayed in him". (KJV)

I'm convinced I went through an AVM so that God's Glory would be displayed in me. Every day that goes by I'm living a normal life. I cook, clean, do laundry, I'm doing things I love like preaching and writing my book.

Nani (great-grandmother) is the only other person that has seen you've changed.

You're right I've changed; I was wounded by what I've had to go through, but God is restoring me. I've had reconstruction surgery with a titanium mesh, and it's as good as or maybe better than having my natural bone. This surgery has allowed me to look like I used to.

Gloria: I don't like that you have a dent on the side of your head.

Getting rid of the dent means risking an infection and risking losing my mesh and that's a risk I'm not willing to take. I love the new me and the dent reminds me of what God has done for me.

Gloria: I feel like the momma I grew up with is gone.

I'm still the same momma. We all change, just like you're changing. It's part of life. Some things about me may have changed after the AVM but I'm still the same momma that loves you and will be here for you always.

My daughter-in-law Nichole's reflection about my AVM

April 6 2017, what started as a normal Thursday afternoon, quickly changed with one phone call from my Father in law, his words, "Your Mother has severe pain in the back of her head and she's vomiting, we're on our way to the ER." My Husband and I showered from work and drove straight to the hospital. When we arrived our father, along with our grandparents, were sitting in the waiting room with worried faces. Our mother was having a MRI done; there was fluid in the back of her brain.

My father in law asked my husband, to take blood pressure medication, to our grandfather who had just been released from the hospital from having a stroke. As we sit there waiting for the results, a hundred and one things are running through my head. What signs has she shown, Fluid? What kind of fluid, Blood? Hemorrhage? Is it an aneurysm? Thank God they made it to the hospital in time to catch it! What's the next step?

Then they call my Father in law back to her room. My husband's grandparents and I sit and wait. Not five minutes go by and my father in law returned to the waiting room, I could see the concern spread across his face. He asks me to come outside, where he tells me its blood and they are sending her in an ambulance to a more equipped hospital to crimp the vein that is bleeding. I hug my Father in law and start to cry.

What does this mean? He says to me, "How do I go in there and tell her parents? Should I tell them? Or should we just go and see what the next hospital says, and then tell them?" I shrug my shoulders still in shock from hearing this God-awful news.

I call my husband and tell him to get here ASAP. Meanwhile my father in law and me, go back to the waiting room, and tell her parents what is happening. My husband arrives, I explained what is going on, and we head to the next hospital.

When we arrive, we were taken to a room in emergency, where finally we get to see her. She is in pain, but awake and talking. She tries to explain what is going on, but she is confused herself. A nurse comes in and tells us, we will be going to the top floor in the neurology department. Once we get in her room, where she spent the next twenty days, the nurses tell us she has arteriovenous malformation a/k/a AVM. "Basically, her blood vessels in her brain are twisted together where they should be flowing freely", a nurse says as she describes the condition.

By this time, it's early Friday morning. They tell us she needs rest. We sit in a small waiting room outside of neurology, dumbfounded, not knowing what to think. My husband and I have not slept in over twenty-four hours at this point. We are exhausted but numb, we just sit in the waiting room researching and taking turns to go see her. They have a strict two people at a time policy, which was hard for us to obey once the whole family arrived.

They allow us all to come into her room, and they show us the 3D scan of her AVM. Her blood vessels looked like an unorganized spider web. They tell us brain surgery is required. The procedure will consist of going in a vein through her inner thigh, up to the part of her brain that's affected, and gluing shut the veins that need to be cut out. On Monday they will do the actual brain surgery, where they will cut open her skull and remove the AVM. Decision time had come. Alongside my husband, father in law, and our grandparents, the doctor asks my mother in law a heart-wrenching question "Do you want to go through with the procedure or take a chance that your brain will hemorrhage again and go home?" I thought to myself, they say it as if it is so simple. They give us some time to talk it over. However, with no hesitation, my Mother in law says, "I'm a child of God; I know and believe all things in him. I'll do this operation in God's hands".

At this point it was late Friday, and none of us had been to sleep or ate anything since Thursday afternoon. We looked and felt like zombies. I finally said, after hours of sitting in the tiny waiting room, we need to eat, shower, and sleep." They agreed. We went to the closest IHOP and ate, booked a room at the closest hotel, showered, slept for about three hours, and back up to the hospital we went before she went back for the first procedure. It is now early Saturday morning, the waiting room is packed (not only with our fifteen family members, but other patient's family members as well) so much so that some of us are sitting in the hallway outside. Sitting in that waiting room trying to see the positive outlook, among chaos from patients being wheeled in and out of neurology, children getting restless running around, and patient's family members calling other family members crying, it was difficult. We came together as a family and prayed.

The time had come. She made it through the first procedure, and we could take our turns going to see her. She looked good, tired but good. Her birthday was the next day, as a family we decided we needed to get together and sing her happy birthday; cake and all. My father in law spoke to the head nurse and they agreed if we weren't disturbing of other patients, we could come in together as a family and spend a short amount of time together with her. Sunday April 9th was one of the most blessed Sundays. We all as a family (If I am remembering correctly, 20 of us) crowded in her small room, sang her happy birthday, ate cake, shared memories, and laughed together. She sang Holy Spirit and the tears began to fall. The moment was short lived, her heart rate started to rise, and we had to leave her to rest. This is where I began questioning, why? Why her? Why now? What if we lost her tomorrow? How would we carry on?

What do you do when the inevitable happens?

Late Sunday night we went back to our hotel. We tried to take our minds off what was occurring the next day, so we played ping-pong in the terrace. After only a couple hours of sleep, it was time to head back up to the hospital, and to give her love and prayers before surgery.

Monday April 10th was horrifying. They explained that her surgery would be around four to six hours all together. We waited as a family in the tiny waiting room as the hours passed by. Hour six came and went, seven, and eight. At this point we were all starting to worry; nobody said anything, but you could tell by our faces. I thought to myself a hundred one times; something is not right. What has happened? Why haven't they informed us on how things are going? Why is it taking so long? Hour nine passed, hour ten, and finally after 11 hours they pushed her through the hallway and back through the neurology doors.

A student nurse came out to speak to my father in law. She was very vague and said there were some complications that her sight might be affected, and she might have some long-term problems. We were confused, what happened? What does that mean? She said the doctor would explain in further detail. My husband and father in law went back to her room while the rest of us waited. About an hour later my husband and father in law came back out, explained they were trying to stabilize her after the surgery, and they were able to do so but now we need to leave her rest. I couldn't help but think the whole way back to the hotel, what are they not saying? What has happened? WHY did it take so long? I stayed quiet; we took showers and fell asleep.

The next day my Father in law spoke to her surgeon. He explained everything we needed to know. AVMs are ranged from stages one to five, with five being the worst. Anything after three they don't do surgery because it's too risky. My mother in laws was a high three, almost a four. The surgeon explained that he has done this surgery more times than he can count, but my Mother in laws was the most complicated he's ever experienced. She suffered a stroke during surgery and that's why it took so long. The surgeon explained that he expected a full recovery, but it was going to be slow, right now she needs rest, and they don't want her heart rate to get too high. My husband and father in law went to see her. They came back quickly, and said she needs to rest her heart rate started to rise, when they went in.

A stroke?

How?

What now?

Can she talk?

Will she be able to walk?

Is she paralyzed?

I started with the questions again. Back to the hotel we went and just waited. We waited for the doctor's call to let us know how she was doing. They had not called so my father in law called, about every hour or so, they would say she is stable and resting. Call after call, same response along with them saying, "No call is good news" not to us. We couldn't wait to hear that she has woken up; little did we know we were far from that day.

After a week of missed work, my husband and I had to return home. We ate dinner with my father in law and told him we were going to stop by the hospital and see my Mother in law before we left. Thinking back now I wish I would've never made that choice. Now remember my husband and father in law, were the only people to see her after her surgery thus far. My husband told me before we entered her room that I needed to be strong, that he couldn't handle saying goodbye for now, and watch me cry. I told him, I'll be strong for you, I won't cry." Lord was I wrong; I took one-step in that room, looked at my mother in law and balled my eyes out. I had to leave, and I went to the waiting room. I waited for my husband to come out, crying and praying alone. My mother in law looked as if someone had beaten her face with a bat. It was the worst thing I have ever seen in my life. I was horrified and started to question whether we were going to make it through this with her. It was a long, silent car ride home. I asked my husband, "I know she looked horrible, is that why you were so quiet?" He replied, "She didn't look like that when Dad and I saw her."

The days went by. We called my father in law numerous times a day to check on him and hear any updates. There was none. On April 26th, twenty days after we began this horrific nightmare, my Mother in law finally opened her eyes. After work my husband and I rushed to the hospital. When we arrived, my father in law said she had just fallen asleep. She looked amazing, compared to how I had last seen her. I was overjoyed just to see the difference in her. We began to talk and rejoice about her waking up. Five minutes later my father in law says to my Husband, "she's looking at you." He held her hand and smiled and they looked at each other for about fifteen minutes straight. My husband said to her, "Nichole is here too." I moved closer to be in her sight and she took her eyes from his and looked in mine. I was so overjoyed at this moment, all my worry faded. God had answered our prayers. No matter what was to come after this, she has woken up, we made it! She quickly shifted her eyes back to my husband; we all laughed and rejoiced the night away.

On May 6th, a month later, she finally spoke! She was transferred from the hospital to a rehab facility. We were in the recovery process. Her left side was affected badly from the stroke. She couldn't move her left arm or leg. She spent a month at the rehab center and was finally able to come home. She still couldn't walk or move her arm, but my father in law was able to get her in and out of bed to shower and use the restroom.

August, they put her skull piece back on, another surgery minor but still surgery. Unfortunately, her body rejected it and an infection started to occur.

They had to remove her skull piece and set a date to implant a cosmetic one. She had to go through another surgery to remove her skull piece, and this was another setback to her healing process.

In October she was having bad stomach pains. Little did we know surgery five would be under way, her gallbladder needed to be removed. Thank God we made it through, we were able to spend the holidays together as a family.

It has been a long hard year, but she has come a long way. She is walking now and getting strength in her arm. She will have her cap replaced in June and be on her way to a full recovery after one, last, final surgery.

I love my mother in law, and I am so thankful to God that she is still here and progressing with each day that goes by. AVM is real and is scary, with strength and power from the lord, we made it through!

SAEBOFLEX

I began searching online; I was looking for products that will help with stroke recovery. Came across Saebo, Inc. Saebo was founded in 2001 by Henry Hoffman and John Farrell. They're headquartered in Charlotte, NC.

Saebo is a global provider of innovative rehabilitation products for stroke survivors and other neurologically impaired individuals. Realizing I fit in their other category; researched Saebo products and was convinced this is something valuable to try.

During one of my therapy sessions at strive Rehabilitation; I spoke with my OT Maria about Saebo and their products. Maria's a hand specialist and I value her opinion. When I shared this with her; she was on-board and said I should contact them. Saebo was polite and easy to deal with; I spoke with one of their therapists and was recommended to use the SaeboFlex. Maria did the training and assessments required by Saebo. They sent a kit of all the resources she needed to order my SaeboFlex. My SaeboFlex test drive unit arrived on August 30th!! It was like Christmas!! An awesome surprise. September 4th therapy session consisted of fitting the SaeboFlex.

This is the beginning of a new chapter that will allow me to gain normal hand function. when we got home; Jorge did a few more adjustments and I began rehabilitative therapy using the SaeboFlex at home. The SaeboFlex is going to be a big blessing; after day one my hand was beginning to loosen its tight grip. It's going to take time to get used to the SaeboFlex; but I know it's benefiting my recovery.

When thirty days were up Saebo informed me; I had to return the unit because insurance approval was pending.

January 16, 2020; great news!

My insurance approved the SaeboFlex!! Best news there's only a 20% co-pay, which makes it affordable! I've learned there's many innovative advancements being made; I'm living in a time where there are many effective therapy devices to help with recovery. I can't give up and must keep pressing forward.

Conclusion

I'd like to wrap it up with this:

We like to paint a picture-perfect world; but who we are is determined by what we do during adversity.

I could've easily painted an AVM survivor picture perfect world for you; but if I did that, I'd be a liar. My Lord wouldn't be content with me. I've had to travel a harsh road; painful enough to feel delirious. At times, wanting to sit in a corner and drown in sorrow. At the beginning of recovery, I embarked on an emotional rollercoaster with no way of getting off. To be honest; there were days I thought I was losing my mind. One day; I was a soaring eagle at the mountain peak. The other day: I was a furious caged animal, mad at the world. My poor husband: I put him through so much! God showed me how to get off my emotional rollercoaster; He used His word to pick me up. I kept thinking of Jesus and Calvary. My AVM is cakewalk when I consider what Jesus endured. This scripture came to my mind in my most depressive moments.

Matthew 16:24 (KJV) "Then said Jesus unto his disciples, if any man will come after me, let him deny himself, and take up his cross, and follow me".

Every step I took towards recovery I'd say, Jesus said to take up my cross and follow him. My AVM and stroke are my cross; therefore, I take up my cross and walk.

I've learned patience and trust.

I say patience because recovery doesn't happen overnight. It's a slow process; going on 4 years and still I have more therapy to do.

I began my AVM journey with fear, fear of death. It got to the point; I didn't want Jorge to leave me alone at the hospital, because I thought if I die, I won't get to tell him goodbye and say how much I love him.

Through time, I've learned "Trust". God knows what's best for me. He's the one who sent me back. The one who keeps me alive; my life is in His hands. I belong to the Lord. He's going to keep me here until His purpose for me is fulfilled. When it's my time to go; He'll receive me in Eternity. My trust is in the Lord; because He takes care of everything I need. He's provided awesome support through my immediate family (parents, husband, sons, daughters in law, and grandchildren). I've been blessed with awesome therapists through every step of recovery.

Philippians 4:19 (NIV)

"And my God will meet all your needs according to the riches of his glory in Christ Jesus".

2 Timothy 1:7 (KJV 1900): For the Spirit God gave us does not make us timid, but gives us power, love, and self-discipline.

The above two scriptures have been a blessing to me through my recovery, specially
2 Timothy 1:7

My Thoughts:

I trust and don't fear.

I've been given Divine power.

I'm loved by God.

I have a sound mind.

2 Corinthians 10:5-6 (KJV)

5 "We demolish arguments and every pretension that sets itself up against the knowledge of God, and we take captive every thought to make it obedient to Christ.

6 And we will be ready to punish every act of disobedience, once your obedience is complete".

I've embraced His word, and I owe Him my success.

I learned with God "**all things**" are possible!

I'm recovering slowly but I'm recovering. I serve a miracle working God who's in the business of restoration. He's an expert of restoring brokenness. There's no doubt he has restored me. I've become dependent on His word. **If He said it, I believe it.** The only thing that's left for me to do is trust Him and walk in His promises for me.

"EMBRACE THE JOURNEY"

Lightning Source UK Ltd.
Milton Keynes UK
UKHW011035210820
368571UK00001B/74